"THE" parade the afterwards--was the crowning point-(ha!)
(Oxford has never seen it's equal for a
Sunday afternoon)

The "LITTLE MAN" IN ONE OF HIS RARE MOODS
(as the genial host at wedding reception of
his niece's (Dean Falkner) wedding, Nov.9/58)
(note how his British features stand out here,
in fact the resemblance here to the late
"Ronald Coleman" is astounding). Cofield

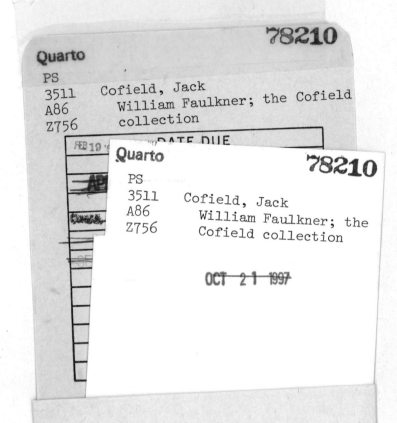

Quarto   78210

PS
3511   Cofield, Jack
A86   William Faulkner; the Cofield
Z756   collection

FEB 19 ...   DATE DUE

Quarto   78210

PS
3511   Cofield, Jack
A86   William Faulkner; the
Z756   Cofield collection

                    OCT 2 1 1997

William Faulkner
The Cofield Collection

To Friend Cofield.   Bill Faulkner

William Faulkner
The Cofield Collection

by

Jack Cofield

Introduction by Carvel Collins

Editing by Lawrence Wells

Art Direction by Barry Mitchell

Layout and Design by William A. Smith

Published by Howard G. Duvall, Jr., and Lawrence Wells

Yoknapatawpha Press

Oxford, Mississippi

Published by Yoknapatawpha Press
Box 248, Oxford, Mississippi 38655

ISBN 0-916242-02-1 LC # 78-54859

Printed in the United States of America

Contents

Preface
by Jack Cofield

By 1973, when Dad locked the doors of his studio for the last time, it had become more of a photographic gallery than a place to have one's portrait made. Every available space was used to display pictures with captions of his favorite subjects: William Faulkner, Oxford and Ole Miss. He even had pictures on the back of the cabinet doors in his workroom (shown on flyleaf pages). Over the years people literally came from around the world to see the collection, expressing interest particularly in the photographs of William Faulkner. From these pictures of Faulkner came the large albums Dad and I put together for the University of Mississippi Library, and from the albums came the idea for the present volume.

The contributors to this book have been listed on the acknowledgements page along with the pages on which their pictures appear. My thanks are due those people and institutions without whose generous assistance this publication would not have been possible. I would like to express special thanks to the Faulkner family for permitting me to use photographs from their own collections: Jill F. Summers, Mrs. John Faulkner, Dean F. Wells, and her mother Louise Meadow. Also, I would like to thank other major contributors for their photographs as well as their suggestions: William Boozer, Aston Holley, Joseph Blotner, Carvel Collins, and my old friend Ed Meek, not only for the use of his excellent photographs, but also for his encouragement and support.

I particularly would like to thank Phil Mullen for the use of his pictures which have proven invaluable, especially since they date from the 1940's. Phil was a long-time friend of William Faulkner, and as editor of *The Oxford Eagle* had occasion to interview and photograph him many times. Words cannot adequately express my gratitude to Phil for his contribution.

A great amount of gratitude is certainly due Robert Linder of the University of Mississippi Library for his help in researching the Mississippi Collection, and Hunter Cole for his suggestions about book design. I would also like to extend gratitude to my colleagues in Public Relations who have helped me in many ways, especially by listening to me talk about this book for two years. I know at times it must have become tedious; thanks for your understanding. I would like to thank Bob Towery and Bill Martin for their untiring help, but most of all I would like to thank my wife, Martha Glenn, whose hard work has truly made this book. The project would have been impossible without her.

Howard Duvall, my publisher and the most enthusiastic Faulkner buff I know, is certainly due a lot of credit. It was he who volunteered to display the Faulkner pictures after Dad closed his studio so that visitors to Oxford might still enjoy the Cofield Collection. From our association, not only has this publication come into being, but lasting friendship and understanding have developed.

In addition to those I have recognized, Dad has asked me to give credit to the late Dorothy Zollicoffer Oldham. Dorothy was Estelle Faulkner's sister, was Curator of the Mississippi Collection, and had a special interest in Rowan Oak after the death of William Faulkner. Through the years, she brought Dad many historical photographs and a large part of Dad's collection is the result of her foresight.

One of the last conversations I had with William Faulkner was in his kitchen at Rowan Oak. The price of cigarettes had just gone up, and I remarked that I just might give up smoking. He rebuked me. "Don't do that," he said. "Don't ever compromise with your pleasures, there are too few of them." Remembering the work sessions with Howard Duvall, Larry Wells, Barry Mitchell, Bill Smith and my wife Martha Glenn, I realize that creating this book has been a pleasure, one that I could not compromise.

Introduction
by Carvel Collins

J. R. ("Colonel") Cofield

J. R. ("Colonel") Cofield of Oxford, Mississippi, by putting his photographic artistry and his collecting instinct at the service of his admiration for William Faulkner, has created an important pictorial history of his town's most famous resident.

Cofield was reared in Cordele, Georgia, where he had been trained by his father and grandfather, both professional photographers. He opened his photographic studio at Oxford in 1928, and that year first met Faulkner, who brought in for enlargement a 1919 snapshot of himself in R.A.F. uniform. Cofield remembers Faulkner's instructions: "Hurry up and copy it so I can put it back in Mother's bureau before she misses it."

During the decades which followed, Cofield became almost an official photographer of Faulkner, and he observes — in "Many Faces, Many Moods" in the volume, *William Faulkner of Oxford* — that his subject was easy to work with: "I always said Bill should have been in Hollywood as an actor, not a writer, because I never saw him fazed by a mere camera. He was so natural that I never had to pose him for any photograph. Everything just fell into place without sweating over getting the right angles."

Cofield began to devote considerable attention to Faulkner well before Faulkner became famous, for he liked his way of life and his style and, especially, his individuality. Though Cofield's natural tendencies as a professional studio photographer — and as a perfectionist besides — somtimes caused him to react against Faulkner's idiosyncracies of dress, he reports in "Many Faces, Many Moods" that he felt differently about Faulkner at their first studio portrait session: "The Associated Press and some periodicals had about worn out the wire between Oxford and New York trying to get some decent pictures of the man. This was in the early thirties, when *Sanctuary* hit the presses, but Bill says, 'No Dice.' That is, till Stell and I ganged up on him. Finally he broke down and told her, 'All right, all right. I'll go down and let Cofield snap a few of me, dammit — but I ain't gonna dress up for it.'...It turned out to be the perfect, plain Bill Faulkner, the home-lovin' man."

Cofield's memories reveal how cooperative the citizens of Oxford were during the Great Depression, a time when they had to depend on each other more than usual. He then acquired a reputation as a morale-booster. Unable, like most people during the Depression, to pay his bills promptly, Cofield did not give conventional excuses to the merchants on the square but instead regaled them with amusing tall tales of inescapable misery. In those hard years others as well as Faulkner came to expect from him wit and determination.

He enjoyed a long acquaintance with Phil Stone, the Oxford attorney who helped Faulkner get his early work published. And he is a close friend of Phil Mullen, for years editor and photographer of the Oxford *Eagle,* who knew Faulkner quite well and provided Cofield with many excellent photographs for his collection.

In addition to making pictures of and for Faulkner, Cofield developed the film which Faulkner shot as amateur photographer. He advised Faulkner about camera technique and later noted in "Many Faces, Many Moods" that Faulkner worked hard to perfect his hobby of photography, though without success: "In the mid-thirties Bill was a devout camera fiend. In his rambles in Europe he had picked up a genuine old Zeiss camera with one of the finest German mechanisms ever made. The only drawback was that you practically had to hold a Georgia Tech degree in order to operate the thing. He'd rush out wildly and shoot up a film and bring it in to me to develop. It usually turned out to be a hodgepodge of double exposures, overtimed or undertimed...He finally gave it up in disgust, even though cameras always did fascinate him."

Cofield is an individualist in his own right, with a flair in publicity for his clients and, at times, for himself. From 1928 to 1958 he made the photographs for the University of Mississippi annual and during all of his professional life was continually involved at the University with football games, beauty contests, fraternity groups, and the University's R.O.T.C. unit. His dedication to publicity for Ole Miss earned him his nickname, after the symbol of school spirit, "Colonel Rebel." One of Cofield's publicity promotions, started partly in fun and partly in admiration for Faulkner, created considerable local attention and some consternation: He proposed after Faulkner's death that Oxford be renamed "Jefferson" for Faulkner's fictional town of that name as well as for Thomas Jefferson and Jefferson Davis. He later said he believed Faulkner would have enjoyed the somewhat angry response of those who took the proposal seriously.

The attention which Cofield has devoted over the years to Faulkner as a man and as a fascinating subject, energetically clipping and copying Faulkner items from magazines and newspapers, making photographs and collecting photographs made by others, and gathering local legends about Faulkner, has culminated in the large albums which he has loaned to the Mississippi Collection in the Ole Miss library, where they have pleased thousands of visitors interested in Faulkner. In compiling those albums "Colonel" Cofield was assisted by his son, Jack, Director of Photography in the University of Mississippi's office for public relations, who also has been in charge of the photographic preparation of this present volume.

The photographs which Cofield has gathered show Faulkner to have been a part of the life of Oxford and Lafayette County yet at the same time detached from it. And they show him to have been closely involved with his family and with a few selected friends. The collection also offers insight into Faulkner's ancestry and into the history of Oxford and Lafayette County during more than half a century, drawing as it does on the work not only of Cofield but of earlier photographers as well. Through his own four decades as a professional in Oxford, Cofield photographed — often on assignment but often for his own pleasure — scenes on the courthouse square, at the University, and in the countryside. And along with any photographs of Faulkner which came to his attention he also stored away copy negatives of local photographs, old and new. This practice may have irritated a few of the owners of such pictures, but the richness of the resulting collection surely offsets that. By following his compelling urge to gather together this sizable body of material about Faulkner, Cofield has done real service, having saved much which otherwise certainly would have been lost.

Differing from some avid collectors, Cofield has always generously shared his collection, making it available to Faulkner's publishers, to photographic journals, to innumerable literary magazines and scholarly and critical publications, to collectors of Faulkner's works and memorabilia, and to any students of Faulkner's life and writing who visited Oxford. For example, from the first time I called on him, in 1948, he has been so generous to me with photographs and information that I am delighted to have been invited to write this introductory note and to have a chance to thank him in print. Always it was "Colonel" Cofield's hope, here being achieved in the ultimate way by the compilation and publication of this volume, that his photographic collection could be available to the world, like the fiction written by its subject, Oxford's extremely photogenic Nobel Laureate.

Studio Portraits

J.R. Cofield recalls the circumstances of his first studio portrait of William Faulkner: "United Press needed a publicity shot for a writeup on *Sanctuary,* Bill's first big success. On this occasion Bill wore an old, old brown tweed coat, red bandana hanky in his pocket, white seersucker pants smeared and spotted with paint, uncombed hair. He objected to the whole procedure (considered it a waste of his valuable time). It took the very best persuasive powers of his wife Estelle and me to get him to perform this feat."

On a hot September day in 1960 Faulkner walked into Cofield's studio to have a passport photo taken. The following spring Faulkner was to visit Venezuela on another State Department trip. As was so often the case, his visit to the studio was impromptu, he gave no advance notice, and he posed in whatever clothes he happened to be wearing at the time. On this occasion he wore a blue cotton workshirt and had just returned to Oxford after having spent the day working at his farm. Cofield comments about the photo on the opposite page, "This is my all-round best shot of Faulkner."

Cofield photographed Faulkner in his riding habit in 1961:

"One morning Bill called me at the house and said, 'Cofield, I'd like for you to take a few shots of me this morning. Some friends of mine up in Virginia are wanting some photographs of me in my riding costume.'

"So I went on down and opened up and got everything all ready. It was a pretty quiet day. Nobody else in the studio. At 10:00 Bill pulled up in his little Rambler station wagon. He commenced taking his riding clothes out of the back of the car.

"He said, 'You got a place I can dress here?'

"I said, 'What kind of outfit is THIS?'

"He didn't say anything. His hair was all groomed and he was clean shaven.

"It didn't take him ten minutes to put his riding habit on. I took one look at him and said, 'My god, what an outfit!' He gave me a genial smile, but he was ready to get on with the picture-making.

"I wanted to pose him with his foot propped on something. Bill spied this little covered stool. I told him to prop his foot up and relax. So he kind of leaned on one knee. I knew that the very first shot, the one Bill posed himself, was the best one, but I shot about a dozen to make sure.

"When Bill came in a day later to see the proofs, he was delighted with them. He immediately picked out the one I thought was the best shot. He was very pleased. It was an honor he was very proud of — riding to hounds in Virginia.

"Later he wrote me several times from Virginia to make him up some extra copies."

8

9

"My son Jack made Faulkner's last studio portraits on March 20, 1962," Cofield recalls. "Jack had always wanted to photograph Bill, so I gave him the keys to the studio, told him to have at it, and went fishing."

The 1962 session yielded a score of pictures which appealed to different people for different reasons. A profile portrait (opposite page) was one of several photos used by sculptor Leon Koury to cast a bust of Faulkner.

Another pose (center) delighted William's wife: "This was Estelle's favorite portrait of Bill," Cofield observes. "When she saw it she remarked that Bill looks like he is smiling down at his grandchildren gamboling at his knee."

Other photographs in the 1962 series revealed that Faulkner habitually kept a box of matches close at hand and carried a handkerchief in his coat sleeve.

The 1962 studio session resulted from a request for a painting of Faulkner. A portrait of him sitting in a chair was chosen as a model for the painting, though Cofield's personal favorite was another seated pose (opposite page). In the upper left-hand corner of the negative he scribbled "IT" in a bold hand.

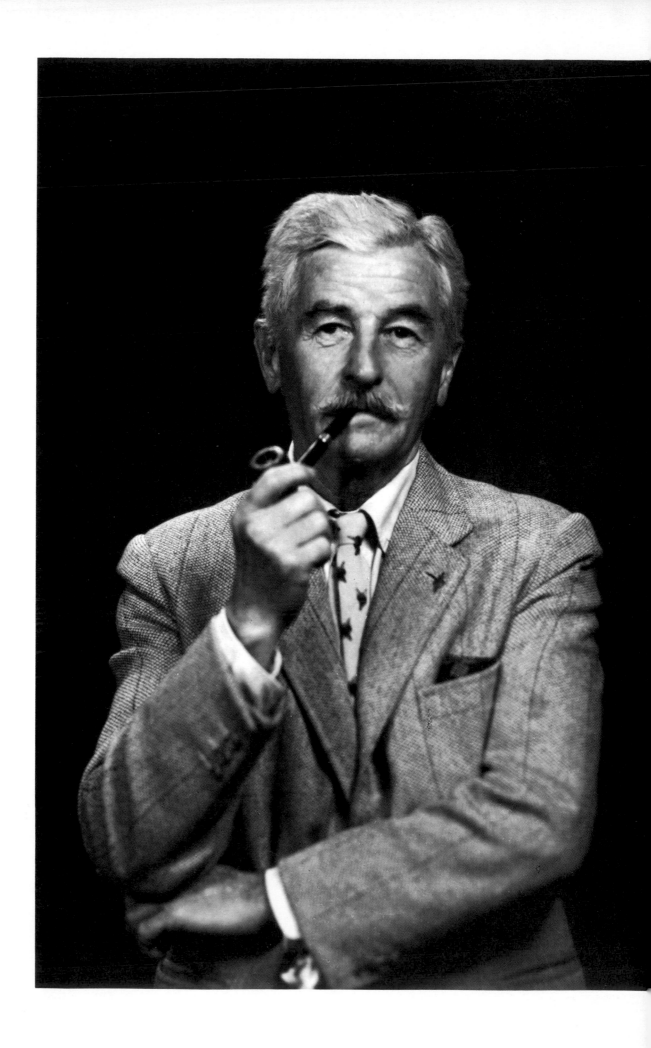

14

William Clark Falkner (1825-1889), William Faulkner's great-grandfather, was a colonel in the Confederate Army during the Civil War. After the war he became a successful planter and businessman. He extended the Gulf & Ship Island Railroad from Middleton, Tennessee, to Pontotoc, Mississippi. He also wrote several books, including *The White Rose of Memphis*, *The Little Brick Church*, and *Rapid Ramblings in Europe*. Colonel Falkner was shot and killed by his former business partner, R.J. Thurmond, as a result of an old feud.

Affectionately known to the family as the "Old Colonel," Falkner designed and built a house in Ripley, Mississippi, with an architectural plan based on a combination of European styles he admired.

A statue of W.C. Falkner in the family plot in the Ripley cemetery looks out over the railroad the Old Colonel built.

17

John Wesley Thompson Falkner
and his wife Sallie Murry were
William Faulkner's paternal
grandparents. Born at Ripley,
Mississippi, in 1848, J.W.T.
moved to Oxford in 1885 and
became an attorney. Cofield
notes, "Photo made in 1910,
same year J.W.T. Falkner
founded the First National
Bank of Oxford and became
its first president."

    J.W.T. Falkner's home, built
in a popular Victorian style, sat
on the corner of University
Avenue and South Street three
blocks from the town square.

The Young Colonel's wife, Sallie Murry, as President of the United Daughters of the Confederacy, led a drive to erect a monument on the square in honor of Confederate soldiers of Lafayette County. Over her strong objections the U.D.C. members decided to place the statue on the University campus. As a result she resigned her office in the U.D.C. and took no active part in commissioning a second statue which was erected on the square in 1907.

A group of Oxford civic officials, photographed in 1910, included J.W.T. Falkner, seated second from right.

Cofield's notes describe a scene photographed on Oxford's square at the turn of the century: "This scene reminds me that the advent of the Ford jalopy broke up a real center of civic interest — the livery stable (and Bill's father, Murry Falkner, ran a popular stable here for some time). Note — the gentleman holding the impatient animal in the foreground is Ben Murray, and the animal is his prize-winning 'jack' named 'Silver Crown.' Also note the architecture — the long porches (which was due no doubt to the need for shade, eh?). The building to extreme left of picture looks much like it does today (Sneed Hardware). It was a dry-goods store at that time. The building to the extreme right of picture is the 'Colonial Hotel' of that day (called The Thompson House). As for the litter in the street around the courthouse, today's city fathers would have groaned with anguish!"

The building which housed Oxford's First National Bank, founded by J.W.T. Falkner in 1910, was photographed sometime after the bank had been moved to another location. Falkner became the bank's first president. His upstairs office overlooking the square was later occupied by a lawyer named Shinault.

Joe Parks was a prominent self-made Oxford businessman and financier who was a member of the board of directors of the First National Bank. On January 13, 1920, Parks and other board members ousted Falkner from office — despite his protests — because of his advanced age. Parks then became president of the bank, with the Colonel's reluctant blessings.

23

On a trip to Memphis in 1911,
J.W.T. Falkner (in white linen
suit and Panama hat) took a
photographer along to record
the success of his new Buick
touring car in negotiating the
bad roads across the Tallahatchie
River bottom. Their first stop
was a general store along the
way. Cofield observes, "No
doubt some of the Colonel's
experiences showed up in
William's last book, *The Reivers*."

24

Cofield continues, "The scene of the stalled auto in the ditch could easily have been 'Hell Creek Crossing' in *The Reivers*. I bet Colonel Falkner was hot as a radiator while waiting for the mules to come pull him out. When they got to the Olive Branch Post Office, the Colonel cooled off in the shade of the porch while his chauffeur, Chess Carothers, had his picture made."

Murry Cuthbert Falkner (1870-1932) bore a close resemblance to his father, J.W.T. Falkner. He also inherited his father's size, standing nearly six feet tall and weighing about 180 pounds. Murry loved his father's Gulf & Ship Island Railroad, where he worked at virtually every position, including fireman, engineer, conductor, vice-president, and treasurer. In addition to his attachment to the railroad, Murry yearned to go west and work as a cowboy. Despite Murry's desire to own and operate the railroad, his father sold it in 1902.

26

William Faulkner's maternal grandmother was Lelia Dean Butler, whom the Falkner children called "Damuddy." Mrs. Butler was acclaimed about town for her artistic talents, especially her practice of the delicate art of buttermolding. Maud Falkner named her youngest son Dean for her mother, who died in 1907 just two months before Dean was born.

An early photograph of Maud Butler (1871-1960) reveals a striking resemblance to her son, William. Cofield observes, "I have always thought William favored his mother more than the other Falkner boys did."

Maud Butler married Murry Falkner in Oxford, Mississippi, on November 7, 1896. Their first home was in New Albany.

Murry had a varied career. He operated his father's railroad in Ripley and New Albany, ran a livery stable and owned a hardware store in Oxford, and later became Business Manager for the University of Mississippi.

Studio photographers Sanders and Sweeney, who took many of the early Falkner family pictures, photographed Maud Falkner in 1896. "I've heard the family say," Cofield remarks, "that Miss Maud always was the only one that could handle Bill when he got on a tear. They said her little black eyes could simply outflash Bill's. I've always believed he got all of his talents from her."

-<|-S ANDERS & S WEENY ,-|<-

OXFORD, MISS.

29

William Cuthbert Falkner
was born in this house in
New Albany, Mississippi,
on September 25, 1897.
Photographed after the family
had moved to Oxford, the house
was situated on the corner of
Cleveland and Jefferson.

30

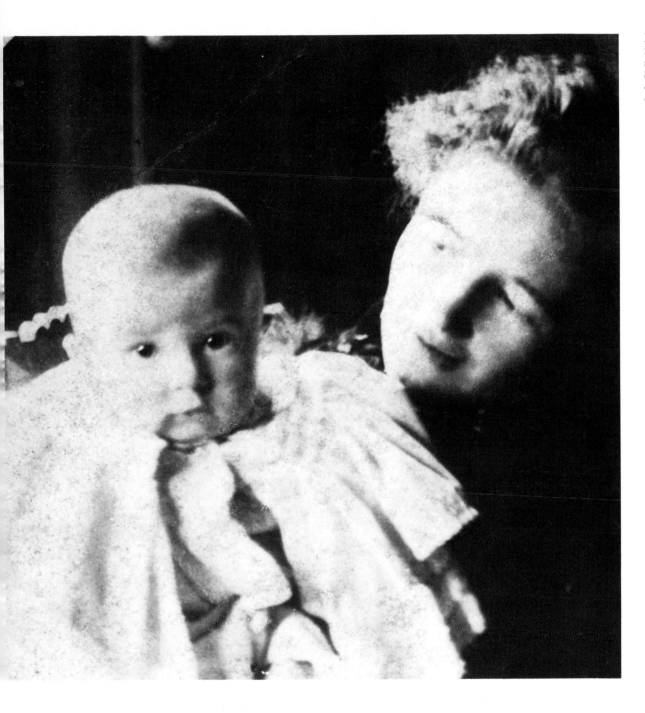

Maud Butler Falkner held her first-born son, William, for a studio portrait by photographer Sweeney. Years later Cofield copied this picture at the request of the family.

In 1898, when William was approximately a year old, another photograph was taken of him, peppermint candy in hand.

"William — age two," notes Cofield. "You can see where the photographer coaxed a little smile from Bill here (his mother called him 'Billy' then and throughout his life). I can tell you from experience, it wasn't easy to get a smiling photograph of William Faulkner!"

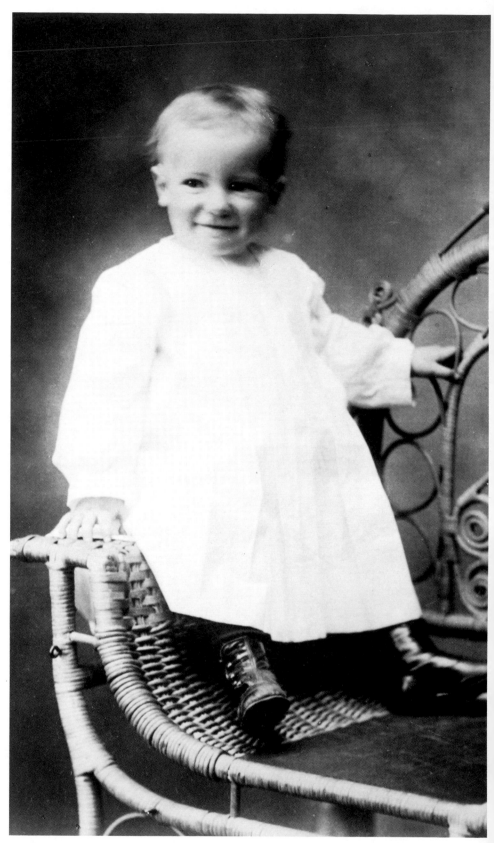

Maud held her second son, Murry, Jr., as two-year-old William looked on. Born at Ripley in 1899, Murry was soon given the nickname Jack.

Maud posed proudly with her third son, John, born September 24, 1901, the day before William's fourth birthday.

William and Jack posed with their baby brother, John, in a studio portrait taken in December, 1903.

35

Dean Swift Falkner, the
youngest of the four brothers,
was born in 1907. His mother,
possibly writing many years
later, incorrectly identified the
photograph as "Billy — 3."

Billy — 3

Cofield comments, "The only picture of all four Falkner brothers — Jack (Murry) at left, William center, John on right, and the baby Dean, picture made in Oxford in 1910. The Boys' nurse, 'Mammy Callie,' gave them the nicknames 'Mimmie' (William), 'Johncy' (John), 'Deanie' (Dean), and 'Jackie' (Jack)."

Cofield observes that the three older Falkner brothers had a hard-won reputation among Oxford youths: "As the saying went, 'Don't pick on one of those Falkner boys unless you can whip all three!'"

Dean Falkner was so much younger than his brothers that he was not able to keep up with them until years later and thus did not share in their reputation for being a tightly knit, tough threesome. The brothers, however, doted on Dean and delighted in playing with him. All his life Dean's special gift for living served as an inspiration for the whole Falkner family as well as a perpetual source of pleasure for them. This cameo of Dean (taken in 1914 for use as a Valentine for Maud's friends and relatives and signed by the photographer, Barrow) was Maud Falkner's favorite, and it hung in her bedroom until her death in 1960.

38

Caroline Barr ("Mammy Callie") came to work for the Falkners as nurse for the children in 1902. A snapshot in 1914 caught Mammy Callie and seven-year-old Dean sitting in the sunshine in front of the Falkner home, shelling black-eyed peas into a basket.

William Falkner's first home in Oxford was photographed in 1905 after the family had lived there three years. Cofield notes, "This is the house Murry Falkner moved his family into when they moved to Oxford from Ripley. It was located a block west of South Lamar Avenue on South 11th Street (then called 'Second South Street'). William is mounted on his spotted pony (left) while Sallie Murry Wilkins (his first cousin) is seated on the steps — Murry C. 'Jack' Falkner, Jr., beside her, holding the white pony, and J.W.T. 'Johncy' Falkner holding the dark pony."

A picture of the Falkner home on Second South Street taken in 1905 during a rare ice-storm was considered so picturesque that it was made into a postcard.

Another picture of the Falkner boys in front of their first home in Oxford showed all three mounted on their ponies: from left, William, Jack, and John.

In the 1909 portrait of the
Sixth Grade Class of the Oxford
Graded School, William
Falkner was sixth from the left
in the back row. Years later,
at the request of a teacher, Miss
Robbie Eades, William
numbered each student in
the photograph and wrote the
corresponding names on the
back.

William received most of his
formal education at the Oxford
Graded School, which was
demolished in the 1960's to make
room for an addition to City
Hall on adjacent property.

POST CARD

CORRESPONDENCE

Hubert Gray   11. Rodney Sisk
O. P. Harris   12. Hugh Lee Simmons
Hal Rushing   13. Neely Dunlap
James Tomlinson   14. Canna Louise McChaney
Donald Funn   15. Victoria Oldham
Wm Falkner   16. Myrtle Ramey
Fielden Webster   17. Mary Paine Wendell
                           18. ANNE whitaway
Duma Black   19. Goodloe Tankersley
Madden Tate   20. Fred Wright

NAME AND ADDRESS

21 Mary Stoner Amy Watt
22
23 Rosa Hargis   34 Wals
24 Ina Houston   Compke
25 annie Grace Banks   32 Jo
26 annie See Mullen   Lee
27 Lunie Holcomb   Linde
28 Mary Stoner
29 Earl McElroy
30 Ralph Markeufuss
31 John Copeland
32 Henry Tate
33 Dawson Mullen

PLACE POSTAGE
STAMP

42

In his eighth grade class portrait, taken in 1911 in front of the Oxford Graded School, William is second from the left in the second row (standing). Cofield notes, "Bill's mother, Miss Maud, wrote all the children's names on the photo."

Murry Falkner moved his family into the house on North Street in 1913. Behind the house was a pasture of fifteen acres. William occupied the upstairs bedroom on the right.

A picture-postcard of North Street showed Oxford's unpaved thoroughfare leading directly to the Murry Falkner home.

"My predecessor in Oxford," Cofield recalls, "fellow by the name of Major (I bought his studio in 1928), took this early shot of South Street where it joined the square. Note the unpaved street in those days. Also Major's 'signature' on his photo — he painted his name with whitewash on the side of the car in left foreground!"

Inside the courthouse, the chancery clerk's office was the seat of much of the town's legal business. A wall calendar attested to the year the photograph was taken.

In 1912 Murry Falkner's livery stable business declined, possibly as a result of the increasing popularity of the automobile. He became affiliated with Relbue Price's Oxford Hardware Company, which stood to the right of Neilson's Department Store on the square. The smaller building was Oxford's fire station, which housed a hand-drawn cart.

Across the street from Murry's hardware store was Goodwin and Brown's Commissary. In his youth William Falkner was a frequent visitor to such stores, with their oiled wooden floors and racks of general goods.

The Oxford Courthouse was pressed into temporary use by the Union Army as a stockade during General Ulysses Grant's sortie through Oxford in 1862. Oxonians were very proud of their first courthouse, which was burned by General A.J. "Whiskey" Smith in 1864, an incident that provoked many local citizens to pass on to their sons an unforgiving attitude toward the "Yankees."

On August 5, 1912, the Lafayette County Confederate Veterans held a reunion at the Methodist Camp Grounds, a traditional gathering place several miles east of Oxford used for church picnics and revival meetings. The veterans ate and drank, spun yarns, and paid tribute to a romantic past. J.W.T. Falkner, proud of his father's career as a C.S.A. Colonel, immensely enjoyed such reunions, as did his sons and grandsons.

William was missing in the last studio portrait of the Falkner brothers: John, Jack, and Dean. A junior in high school, William was beginning to find many interests outside the close family circle, such as the picnic gathering where he was photographed with a guitar in his hands (though it is doubtful that he could play the instrument).

49

In high school William fell in love with Estelle Oldham, whose family had moved to Oxford in 1903. Her father, Lem Oldham, was U.S. Circuit Court clerk, and their home was located on South Street. When Estelle began wearing William's school ring, her parents expressed disapproval of him because of his desire to become a writer rather than pursue a more conventional career. Accordingly, the Oldhams encouraged Estelle to date other young men.

Although Estelle Oldham's picture (opposite page) appeared in the 1913 yearbook *Ole Miss* as a member of a social club, the "Outlaws," her name was not listed on any class roll that year. Directly above her photograph in the club picture was that of the man she would marry five years later, Cornell Franklin. A law student with political ambitions, Franklin was a senior at the University of Mississippi in 1913, and his list of accomplishments showed him to be an extremely well-rounded and distinguished student.

Roberson   Pound   Miller   Franklin

Anne Fowlkes   Minnie Ethel Lombard   Era Coney   Estelle Oldham

The residence of "General" James Stone was the scene of many earnest literary discussions between William Falkner and his friend and supporter, Phil Stone. An avid reader keenly interested in current literature, Phil became acquainted with William in 1914, having heard that sixteen-year-old William was serious about writing poetry.

In the spring of 1918 Phil Stone was enrolled in the Yale Law School when Estelle Oldham's parents announced her engagement and pending marriage to Cornell Franklin. Knowing of William's desire to avoid the wedding festivities, Phil invited him to New Haven for an extended visit. William got a temporary job as clerk at the Winchester Arms Company and soon began to seek enlistment in the R.A.F.

Apprentice

In July, 1918, William Faulkner was enrolled as a cadet in the R.A.F. at Toronto. On the preceding page he is pictured in his cadet uniform. After the Armistice, Faulkner returned to Oxford in December, 1918. At home he posed for a photograph in the uniform of an R.A.F. Lieutenant, a rank he never attained. Here, as in many pictures, he used a cigarette as a prop and did not look straight into the camera.

55

In another military pose, ex-cadet Faulkner, obviously enjoying the charade, was photographed with Sam Browne belt and close-fitting cap.

The next year (1919) William enrolled at the University of Mississippi, where his father, Murry C. Falkner, had accepted the position of Assistant Secretary (business manager). Murry's office was located in the Lyceum, the University's administration building.

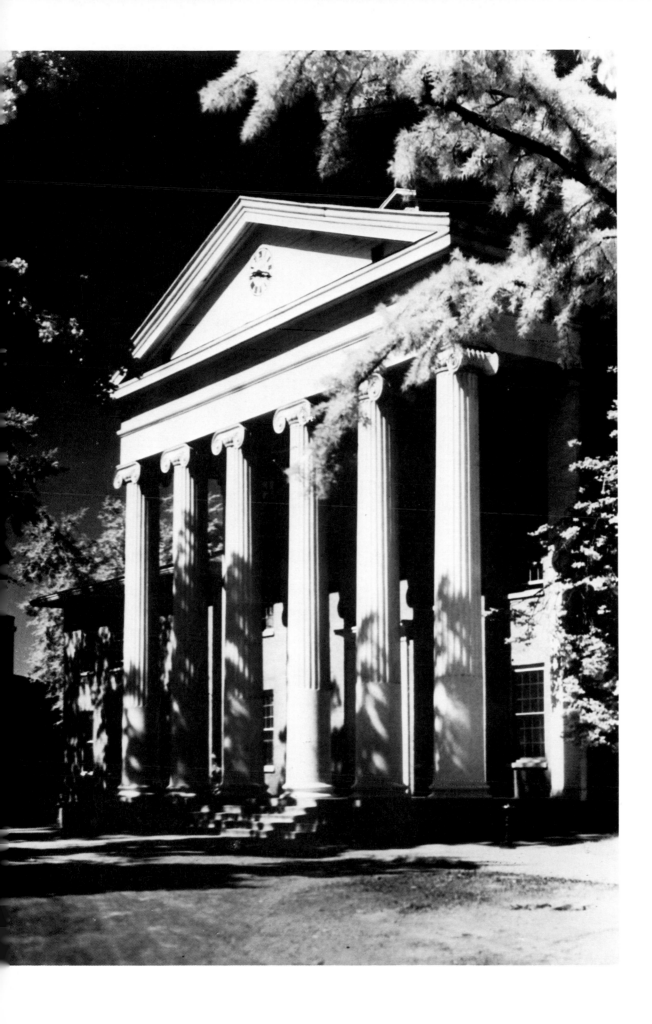

The Falkner home on the university campus had once been occupied by the Delta Psi Fraternity. William lived here for a time with his parents and youngest brother, Dean, who at age twelve found his older brother's room in the tower a haven where William would tell him stories and draw pictures of football players, trains, and horses.

The gates of the University of Mississippi were a familiar landmark to the Falkner family, because the street under the arch led past their new home.

In 1919 Faulkner was photographed with his fraternity Sigma Alpha Epsilon (back row, far right). As a special student — one not seeking to meet graduation requirements — he soon acquired a reputation on campus as an indifferent scholar in the classroom yet imaginative and talented outside it. He was eagerly sought after by his literary-minded classmates for his creative abilities, especially as poet and sketch-artist. At twenty-two he was slightly older than most students and had established an identity as "Count" William because of his sartorial affectations and his regal disdain of consequent criticism. An anonymous wag listed Faulkner in the freshman class roll in the 1920 *Ole Miss* as "Falkner, Count William."

Faulkner was active in the student drama club, The Marionettes, which he helped establish with his friends, Ben Wasson and Lucy Somerville. Although William's picture was not included with the others in the 1921 *Ole Miss,* he was listed in the membership roll as property man.

In 1920 Faulkner wrote a one-act play entitled "Marionettes," which was never produced because it was considered too risque for university audiences. Faulkner laboriously hand-lettered, illustrated, and bound six copies of his "first book," and sold them to friends for five dollars each. The text reveals the young poet's characteristic neatness and his habit of using curious, inverted *S's.* He signed his play "W. Faulkner," as he had occasionally begun to add a *u* to his name as early as 1918.

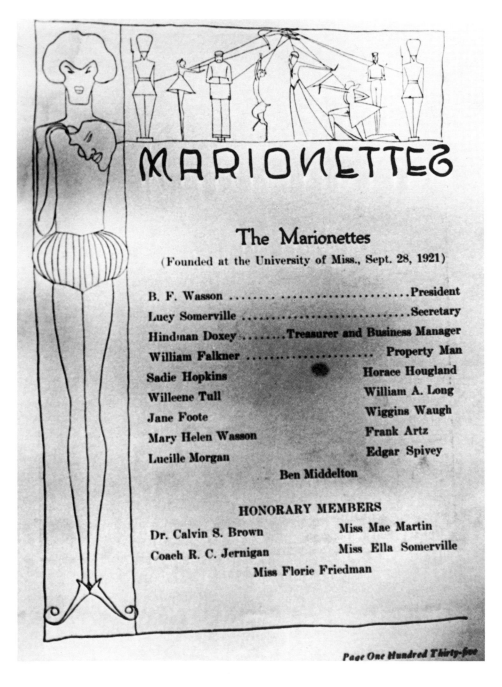

MARIONETTES

The Marionettes

(Founded at the University of Miss., Sept. 28, 1921)

B. F. Wasson ....President

Lucy Somerville ....Secretary

Hindman Doxey ....Treasurer and Business Manager

William Falkner .... Property Man

Sadie Hopkins   Horace Hougland

Willeene Tull   William A. Long

Jane Foote   Wiggins Waugh

Mary Helen Wasson   Frank Artz

Lucille Morgan   Edgar Spivey

Ben Middelton

HONORARY MEMBERS

Dr. Calvin S. Brown   Miss Mae Martin

Coach R. C. Jernigan   Miss Ella Somerville

Miss Florie Friedman

Page One Hundred Thirty-five

and he stops against the sky; perhaps his

heart also misgives him. He stops, half turned

toward her, and for a fleeting second, he is

the utter master of his soul; fate and the

gods stand aloof watching him. his destiny

waits wordless at his side. Will he turn

back where she awaits him in her rose

bower, or will he go on? He goes on, his

eyes ever before him, looking into the implac-

able future. Perhaps a newer, stronger love

has called him away, that he does not re-

turn; perhaps he is fallen upon by

William posed with the American Legion Club in the 1920 *Ole Miss*. On the third row he is second from the left, and his brother Jack is fourth from the left. As the enlarged detail discloses, Faulkner expressed his individuality by resting an umbrella carelessly on his shoulder and by smoking a cigarette in a slim holder.

In the university yearbook, Faulkner is listed as a member in the A.E.F. Club, though he never served overseas. He did, however, draw illustrations for the A.E.F. Club roster under the signature "W Falkner."

Le grand   Americaine Parlez-vous Anglais, mam'zelle?
La petite Francaise — Mais oui, m'sieur, un peu; Do you love me? Kees me queek! Damn! 'ell!

Members of A. E. F. Club

The military influence on campus social life was reflected in town by patriotic celebrations such as a D.A.R. convention photographed on the square in the early 1920's. While a crowd on the courthouse lawn listened to a speech, D.A.R. members seated in a decorated car were attended by veterans of two wars: the driver in his W.W.I uniform and the mounted horseman wearing Confederate gray.

63

A picture of the Illinois Central Railroad Depot revealed, as Cofield observes, "the hustle and bustle of students arriving on the campus which was just up the hill from the depot. The photo was taken about the time that William was attending Ole Miss — around 1919-20."

A local postcard in the early 1900's featured the old wooden bridge at the entrance to the university campus, just south of the railway depot. The Falkner house was located only a few hundred yards from the railroad tracks, and William and his brother Dean spent many happy hours leaning out the upstairs window at night, vying to see who could correctly guess which engineer was at the controls. From their father all four Falkner boys had inherited a love of trains, and each knew many engineers of the Illinois Central not only by name but by their distinctive touch on the train whistle.

64

One of several cartoons Faulkner drew while he was a student at the university depicted a dance featuring W.C. Handy's famous jazz band. "Bill Faulkner not only was the best observer and listener I ever knew," Cofield recalls, "but he was fully capable of sketching everything he saw as well as writing about it. His drawing of W.C. Handy, 'The Blues Master of Memphis,' typifies exactly the Roaring Twenties at Ole Miss — era of the 'hip-pocket flask,' the 'raccoon coat,' and the 'iron steed' awaiting without (namely the Stutz Bearcat)."

65

Faulkner's illustrations for A.E.F. Club pictures in the 1921 yearbook suggest the presence of many young World War I veterans who had returned to their studies at the university.

For the "social activities" picture in the 1920 *Ole Miss* he drew a woman dancing with a clown figure reminiscent of the French Pierrot, a character which held Faulkner's interest at the time and which he featured in his illustrated play, "Marionettes."

FISH, FLESH, FOWL

SOCIAL ACTIVITIES

A.E.F. CLUB

THINK HOW MANY TIMES THIS BIRD'S BEEN KISSED. HE GOT A CROIX DE GUERRE, WITH PALMS.

In the summer of 1920, when Faulkner earned money by doing odd jobs, he painted the University Law Building. At one point during the project, he dangled from the steeple by a rope in order to paint otherwise inaccessible places.

Murry C. (Jack) Falkner, Jr., a Marine veteran who was wounded near the Argonne Forest, enrolled in the University after the war. In the 1922 *Ole Miss,* the caption under his picture as a senior law student reads, "Falkner always speaks to the point, argues forcibly, reasons clearly and logically, ruling out irrelevant and immaterial matter."

Faulkner took the position of Postmaster at the University Post Office in December, 1921. The work was predictably monotonous, and he soon acquired a reputation for careless treatment of the mail. He reportedly spent a great deal of time playing poker, reading, sketching, or writing during working hours. In 1924, his indifferent attitude caught up with him when the postal authorities asked for his resignation. After he resigned, Faulkner succinctly explained his feelings about the duties of a postmaster: "I refuse to place myself at the beck and call of every S.O.B. with the price of a two-cent stamp."

A drawing by William during his tenure as Postmaster elicited an observation from Cofield: "Bill could have gone far as an artist, the talent inherited no doubt from his mother's side of the family (the Butlers), as both Miss Maud and her mother were gifted artists. The drawing Bill called 'Post Office Blues' is his imaginative sketch of Lottie Vernon White (later Mrs. Guy Turnbow) and himself dancing by the Victrola in December, 1923."

POST OFFICE BLUES

68

In the early 1920's Faulkner served as leader of a local Boy Scout troop. He took his scouts camping and taught them woodlore. Often he and his troop would hike to Thacker's Mountain (elevation 623 feet), four miles southwest of Oxford, where the scouts would make camp under blackjack oaks and listen to Faulkner's ghost stories around the fire at night. Although William was very popular with his scouts, he was asked to resign because of rumors about his drinking.

Phil Stone's law office in Oxford was the scene of many visits between Faulkner and his friend and confidante. In May, 1924, they mailed the manuscript of a book of verse to the Four Seas Company and negotiated with them for private publication at a fee of $400.00. Faulkner and Stone later went to friends and acquaintances around Oxford, selling them copies of Faulkner's first published book, *The Marble Faun.*

Accepting the advice of his friends, Ben Wasson and Phil Stone, Faulkner left Oxford in 1925 for what turned out to be an extended stay in New Orleans and its bohemian artist colony. He began to sell articles and stories to the *Times-Picayune*, and he became the friend of artist William Spratling, with whom he later collaborated on a book.

Spratling also sketched William's portrait.

When he arrived in New Orleans, Faulkner stayed for some time at Sherwood Anderson's apartment in the upper Pontalba Building on Jackson Square in the French Quarter.

70

On July 7, 1925, Faulkner and Spratling sailed for Europe aboard the freighter *West Ivis*. After traveling through Italy, Switzerland, and France, Faulkner lived in Paris for a few months among the American expatriate writers and artists on the Left Bank. He worked on his novel *Soldier's Pay,* which was published soon after his return to America. W.C. Odiorne photographed him sitting at his favorite place in the Luxembourg Gardens in Paris.

In the summer of 1926 Faulkner vacationed with the Stone family at their home at Pascagoula, Mississippi. During the long, quiet afternoons, Faulkner sat with his battered portable typewriter on a bench in the yard, and, with the Gulf of Mexico in the background, worked on his second novel, *Mosquitoes* (published 1927).

72

His former sweetheart, Estelle Oldham Franklin, was living in Shanghai, where she was photographed with her daughter, Victoria. Estelle's family-arranged marriage to Cornell Franklin was not working, and she was in the habit of making regular trips home to Oxford. In 1927 Estelle returned home for good, having filed for a divorce.

In April, 1929, Estelle's divorce decree was granted, and William began to court her again, playing daily with her two children, Victoria, ten, and Malcolm, five, and becoming a favorite of theirs. On June 20, 1929, William and Estelle were married in the Presbyterian Church at College Hill, four miles northwest of Oxford.

William's mother- and father-in-law, Lida and Lem Oldham, had been opposed to William's courtship of Estelle in 1918. Eleven years later, however, they acquiesced to the idea of William's marrying their daughter.

74

Faulkner accepted the advice of Sherwood Anderson to write about "that little patch" of native soil which he knew the best. For the next two years he lived in Oxford, with occasional stays in New Orleans or New York, writing furiously and completing two novels, *Sartoris* and *The Sound and the Fury* (both published in 1929). The Chandler house, three blocks from Faulkner's childhood home on South Lamar, has been thought a model for the fictional Compson house in *The Sound and the Fury*.

Ben Wasson was Faulkner's literary agent in New York and negotiated the sale of *Sartoris* with the publisher, Harcourt, Brace. Wasson edited the long and complex manuscript (originally entitled *Flags in the Dust*) for publication, cutting much material in order to tighten the plot.

75

When William and Estelle returned to Oxford after spending the summer in Pascagoula, William took a job on the night shift at the University power plant. He brought the fireman coal to keep the furnaces going. During the long intervals when the coal bins were full and there was nothing to do, Faulkner worked on his next novel, *As I Lay Dying,* with a wheelbarrow as his desk and the deep hum of a dynamo in the background.

William and Estelle made a home for themselves and the children, Victoria and Malcolm, in an apartment on the first floor of Miss Elma Meek's house on University Avenue. In addition to the novel *As I Lay Dying,* Faulkner wrote one of his most famous short stories, "A Rose For Emily," in this house. He and his family lived here from the fall of 1929 until June, 1930, when they moved to the antebellum home Faulkner would later call "Rowan Oak."

Struggling Writer

In 1930, Faulkner moved his family into the Old Bailey Place, which he had purchased, along with four acres of land, from Sallie Bailey Bryant for a reported $6,000.00. The deteriorating antebellum mansion had been built around 1844 by Colonel Robert Sheegog, and the general state of disrepair of the house, which lacked plumbing or electricity, provided a challenge for William's practical skills. Working beside the carpenter he hired, Faulkner put up screens, installed wiring and pipes, papered and painted walls, and reshingled the roof. He also built a front gallery and a *porte cochere*. And he named his new home Rowan Oak after a Scottish legend which holds that a branch of the tree, when nailed to the front door, will keep out witches and other evil spirits.

At a time when journalists were beginning to be intimidated by Faulkner's growing reputation as a recluse who refused to grant interviews, Marshall J. Smith, a writer-photographer from the Memphis *Press-Scimitar,* bravely arrived unannounced at Rowan Oak on a sunny day in August, 1931. His initiative was rewarded with an interview and photographs of the author with corncob pipe.

A young and hardy Faulkner proudly displayed his kitchen garden to Smith. For the next thirty years vegetables would be grown virtually year-round in this garden, maintained, for the most part, by the family servants who occupied a small frame house behind Rowan Oak.

Faulkner also cultivated a grape arbor (scuppernong vines) and occasionally made wine. He told Smith (as reported in Smith's article published in *The Bookman*, December, 1931) that he had not written a "real novel" yet, because he was "too young in experience." He hoped that in five years he could "put it over" and write "a *Tom Jones* or *Clarissa Harlowe.*"

With newspaper in hand and tongue in cheek, Faulkner posed in front of his outhouse at Rowan Oak, belying the fact that indoor plumbing had at last been installed.

Sitting in a canvas chair behind a writing table, Faulkner posed with a proprietary air in front of his new home. Whether or not the photograph was intended to portray the author actually at work, it conveys an idyllic sense of peace, beauty, and isolation. The young writer had created for himself and his family the beginnings of a stately, graceful, Southern lifestyle. Determined to support his ideal way of living, Faulkner had submitted 37 short stories to magazines in the past year, though he had sold only six of them.

An anecdote by Cofield illustrates the fact that everyone in Oxford shared the hard times of the early thirties: "Mac Reed told me about a ten-dollar gold piece that Bill brought to Mac to pawn during the real lean years of the Depression. Mac said he let him have the ten bucks but told him he did not want to keep the gold piece. But Bill insisted, and later paid back the loan promptly. Bill was just that exacting in his business affairs where his friends were concerned."

In 1931, Faulkner's national reputation was given impetus by the publication of his sensationalistic novel *Sanctuary*, and he began to sell more stories to such major magazines as *Scribner's* and *Saturday Evening Post*. His royalties enabled him to continue to maintain Rowan Oak, make house payments, and provide for his family.

Some scenes in *Sanctuary* were set in Memphis, a city that Faulkner knew well. A 1925 photograph of Memphis' Main Street shows the bustle of city life so different from the quiet of Oxford 85 miles away. In the 1920's and 30's, William and his brothers often drove to Memphis to enjoy the night life the city offered.

One of Faulkner's favorite places in Memphis was the Peabody Hotel. He concurred with (fellow writer) David Cohn's observation that "the Mississippi Delta begins in the lobby of the Peabody Hotel in Memphis and ends on Catfish Row in Vicksburg."

An aerial photograph of the Memphis skyline included the wide and muddy Mississippi River and the Memphis-Arkansas bridge.

87

In the hard times of 1930 and
'31, when the Bank of Oxford
closed and everyone felt the
pinch of the Depression,
Faulkner was writing furiously
to support his family, repeatedly
sending stories out to magazines
after they had been rejected. In
the winter of 1930-31 he had
additional cause to earn money:
Estelle was expecting a child.

On January 11, 1931, William and Estelle's first child, Alabama, was born two months prematurely. When Faulkner brought his wife and infant daughter home to Rowan Oak, the family proudly agreed that Alabama's tiny features resembled "Bill's." The frail baby became ill, however, and William and his brother Dean rushed to Memphis to acquire an incubator. Despite all efforts, the infant died January 20. A funeral service was held at Rowan Oak, attended by immediate family members and several close friends. With the small casket in his lap, William rode to St. Peter's Cemetery, where Alabama was buried in the family plot. He later donated the incubator to the local hospital.

While William continued to meet family responsibilities, publishing in 1931 a collection of stories, *These 13*, his brother Dean continued to provide the whole Falkner family with pleasure and entertainment. Always the athlete, Dean tried out for the Ole Miss baseball team in his freshman year. He is seated on the back row, second from left, in the yearbook picture of the team.

In May, 1932, Faulkner was hired by Metro-Goldwyn-Mayer Studio for the first of many contract writing assignments in Hollywood. During his first trip to Los Angeles, a friend took him on a short sightseeing tour of the Red Rock Canyon where this photograph was made. Two months later, on August 7, 1932, Murry Falkner died; and William returned to Oxford to assume responsibility as head of the family. In the near future he would support at least nine people, including his mother and Dean as well as Estelle, Jill, Malcolm and Victoria, and the servants at Rowan Oak. Although he found writing screenplays for Hollywood studios to be hack work, he returned to Los Angeles many times in the years to come in order to earn the wages necessary to support his family.

Faulkner wrote the screenplay for the film "Today We Live" in 1932, in addition to publishing *Light in August* and *Miss Zilphia Gunt.* The "world premiere" of the movie was held at the Lyric Theatre in Oxford on April 12, 1933. Faulkner gave a short address to the excited audience. The film starred Gary Cooper and Joan Crawford, and admission was 35 cents for adults, 25 cents for children.

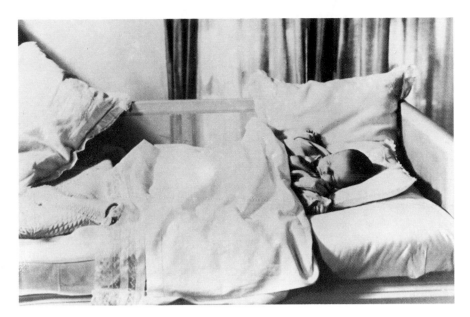

William and Estelle's daughter Jill was born on June 24, 1933. Faulkner proudly brought Estelle and the baby home to Rowan Oak.

The following winter Faulkner posed with Jill on the steps of Rowan Oak. He had told friends and relatives that he wanted the baby to be a girl. He was a doting father and heartifully enjoyed playing with his daughter.

Cofield photographed Jill Faulkner's first birthday party on June 24, 1934. He comments, "Bill's wife, Estelle, called me to get me to take a picture of little Jill's party. Jill is far right, with her nurse, and my little daughter, Tommye Jane, is second from left (with her finger in her mouth — she always was the shy one)."

THE FIRST BIRTHDAY Party given by Mrs. Bill Faulkner for her daughter "Jill".

...ndra Williams, Tommye Jane, Bobbie Little, Baxter Elliott, Mildred Douglass, Jill Faulkner, standing, Baby Little, laying down, Leighton Pettis, Jr. (Hurtis)

Faulkner began taking flying lessons from Vernon Omlie at the Memphis airport in 1933, thus fulfilling a desire born during his brief training in the R.A.F. The next year, having published *Dr. Martino and Other Stories*, Faulkner bought an airplane, a 210 H.P. Waco C Cabin Cruiser. His pride of ownership produced a rare, broad grin.

According to Jack Falkner, the picture of William in flight jacket and silk scarf (opposite page) was made at the Oxford airport in 1933.

In 1935, John Falkner became a commercial pilot, flying with J.O. Dockery of Clarksdale, Mississippi. At William's urging, his youngest brother, Dean, also became a licensed pilot, flying air charter service for Vernon Omlie's Mid-South Airways Company as well as performing aerial acrobatics for Omlie's flying circus.

Jack Falkner, also a pilot as well as a highly successful F.B.I. agent, was photographed with J. Edgar Hoover in Rosewell, New Mexico, in 1937. All four Falkner brothers flew so often in the mid-thirties that their mother once quipped, "I don't have a son on earth!"

John Falkner and his sons Chooky and Jimmy were photographed beside John's charter plane at the Clarksdale airfield in 1935.

Promising "three hours of thrilling, death defying entertainment" for twenty-five cents, a poster proclaimed John Falkner's participation in a flying circus scheduled for a performance in Greenwood, Mississippi, in 1935.

Al Gardner Presents

J.O. Dockery, Barney Root, Hugh Mitchell

THE FAMOUS FLYERS

John Falkner III

Nationally Known Flying Organization

in a Thrilling Exhibition of

DARE-DEVIL STUNTING, RACING AND PARACHUTE JUMPING

SUNDAY, 2 P. M. AT GREENWOOD AIRPORT

Three Hours of Thrilling, Death defying entertainment

SEE an Airplane loop, roll and spin with the motor completely cut off.

SEE Thrilling race between airplane and FORD V-8 Automobile.

SEE an Airplane flying inverted within 50 feet of ground.

SEE Death defying delayed parachute jump, jumper falling 2000 feet before opening chute.

SEE Upside down stunting and the dangerous outside loop.

SEE Dead stick landings, bomb dropping at moving target, formation stunting and actual army combat maneuvers.

Positively the Most Thrilling and Sensational Air Show ever presented in this section of the Country. (Sponsored by the American Legion.)

ADMISSION 25c   **CHILDREN 10c**

FREE PARKING

In case of inclement weather Show will be held the following Sunday.

Taking a break from his work,
Faulkner relaxed in his library
at Rowan Oak. Very few pictures
were taken of him in so casual
a pose.

Dean Swift Falkner was killed on November 10, 1935, in the plane William had given him. With him were several passengers, one of them a student-pilot who was thought to have been practicing at the controls when the plane crashed near Thaxton, Mississippi. Dean's death was an irreparable loss for the family, and William felt partially responsible because he had urged Dean to become a pilot.

Dean was buried in the family plot at St. Peter's Cemetery. William assumed responsibility for all funeral arrangements, including the inscription on his brother's tombstone. From his novel *Sartoris* William took the epitaph of the fictional pilot, John Sartoris, who also died in a plane crash: "I bare him on eagles' wings and brought him unto me."

At an airfield seven miles south of Oxford, Faulkner (far right) joined a group of aviation supporters who greeted record-setting pilot Al Key (center, arms folded) in 1936.

In another picture taken the same day, Faulkner was photographed hat in hand, bandana handkerchief crammed into breast pocket. The events of the day would have stirred memories of his brother, Dean, who had flown out of that airfield many times.

100

Early Success

Under the awning on Maud Falkner's gallery, ninety-six-year-old Mammy Callie rocked the last of her Falkner infants on her stiffly starched lap. Affectionately called "Dean-baby" by the family, the child was born four months after her father's death. William assumed legal guardianship of little Dean and became a father to her.

The airfield south of Oxford was dedicated as the Dean Falkner Memorial Airport on May 19, 1938. Present at the ceremony were Dean's widow, Louise Hale Falkner, and her two-year-old daughter, as well as many friends, including pilots from St. Louis and Memphis with whom Dean had flown.

Jill Faulkner's third birthday party was held at Rowan Oak in June, 1936. Faulkner children, friends, and family servants assembled on the front gallery to watch her blow out the candles. From left: Malcolm Franklin, William's stepson; Chooky, John's son; Xandra Williams, a cousin; Cherry Sisk; Jill; Holland Williams, a cousin; and Jimmy, John's elder son.

An enthusiastic amateur photographer, Faulkner posed Mammy Callie and four-year-old Jill beside a storeroom where he kept harnesses, saddles, and tools. On the back of the finished print he carefully noted lens setting, shutter speed, and date (1937). Three years later Caroline Barr died at the age of one hundred. William conducted her funeral at Rowan Oak and later dedicated the book *Go Down, Moses* to her.

104

Cofield photographed the "private" sign which William himself painted and erected at the entrance to his driveway. He notes, "This was Bill's first small sign—later when he built his gateway, he put up a huge one in box car letters you could read a block away." Faulkner's demand for privacy denoted the fame he was beginning to achieve in the late 1930's. His first major financial coup was the sale of *The Unvanquished.* In February of 1938, Random House published the novel and sold the screen rights to M.G.M. for $25,000.00. With his share of the profits, Faulkner had at last achieved some respite in his constant financial struggles, and now he was able to write at a more leisurely pace.

105

On Sunday morning, May 8, 1938, Faulkner telephoned Cofield and asked him to come to Rowan Oak to take some pictures. He and his friends Ross Brown and Colonel Hugh Evans had brought home venison and quail from a hunt and had decided to hold a hunt breakfast. No one would be allowed to attend unless mounted and dressed. Resplendent in polished boots, fawn-colored breeches, ruffled shirt and velvet jacket, grey gloves and huntsman's cap, Faulkner greeted his guests with a short blast at the hunting horn around his neck and served them straight bourbon in shot glasses. Cofield recalls, "Bill's butler had his standing order to serve jiggers of 'Old Forester' every fifteen minutes or so. I had to beg off after a couple of jiggers. Told Bill to make his man pass me up—I was starting to see two of everything. Depicted from left to right: (front row) Dr. Bell Wiley, in 'Coat of Mail', Nina Culley, Minnie Ruth Little, Mary Frances Wiley, Bob Williams, Col. Hugh Evans, Sallie Murry Williams, Mary Evans, Maggie Brown, Ross Brown, and Dr. John Culley; (back row) Bill Faulkner, butler Ned Barnett, Estelle and wee daughter Jill, and family servants."

106

Dan Brennan, a young man from Minnesota, visited Faulkner at Rowan Oak in May, 1940. Faulkner had a writing schedule to meet that day, and while Brennan browsed in Faulkner's library, the author sat at his typewriter and worked on a draft of the short story "Go Down, Moses." Faulkner's most recent major publications prior to that time had been *The Wild Palms,* 1939, and *The Hamlet,* 1940.

Faulkner's library was both a family room and a writing room. In the summer the high-ceilinged room in the old house was cool and quiet. In the winter a cozy wood fire burned in the fireplace.

Brennan posed with his host and Jill on the front steps of Rowan Oak. Though Faulkner had told Brennan he was "suffering from insomnia lately," he was a gracious and patient host, a fact Brennan acknowledged in an article published fifteen years later.

Faulkner and Jill were photographed as they strolled up their brick walk lined with cedars.

Faulkner's Ford touring car was parked to the rear of the house, beneath the *porte cochere*. Behind the house Faulkner had planted a miniature formal garden, complete with closely trimmed hedges and a gazebo built of oak slats.

Brennan took a snapshot of Faulkner, drink in hand, relaxing on his front gallery. Earlier that day Faulkner had set up his writing table and typewriter in his garden. Apparently Faulkner occasionally followed the practice of writing outdoors, surrounded by the peace and beauty of his four-acre, wooded grounds. At lunchtime, Estelle served sandwiches in the shade of the east gallery. Before Brennan left, William and Estelle posed for him on the front steps of Rowan Oak.

A picture taken in front of John Faulkner's home in 1941 included most of the family. Left to right: (first row) Chooky, Dean, and Jimmy; (second row) Holland Falkner Wilkins, Maud Falkner, J.W.T. Falkner, Jr. (William's uncle), his wife Sue; (third row) Lucille Faulkner, her husband John, Dean's widow, Louise; also shown are family servants, Minnie Bell and Gene Harkins.

John Faulkner, generally conceded to be the handsomest of the four brothers, was a talented artist and writer. From his experience with the Works Projects Administration, John wrote a novel entitled *Men Working*, published in 1941 to good reviews.

A photograph of a W. P. A. sign provided ideal publicity for John's first book.

In 1941 a *Life* magazine photographer came to Oxford to photograph and interview John. Maud, proud to have another published writer among her sons, posed with her "Johncy."

John Faulkner's *Dollar Cotton*, a novel about a planter's empire in the Mississippi Delta, was published in 1942.

113

After having unsuccessfully
applied for a commission in the
U.S. Naval Reserve, Faulkner
began a series of writing
assignments for Warner
Brothers in 1942. When Estelle
and Jill came to California for
an extended visit, William often
took Jill riding at Glendale
Stables.

At a gathering of Warner Brothers staff in 1943, Faulkner was photographed with Ruth Ford. They were old friends, having met when Miss Ford was a student at the University of Mississippi.

During World War II, Jack Falkner served in U.S. Intelligence, attaining the rank of major. In 1943, while serving in North Africa, he met his future wife, Suzanne, a French-Algerian. A year later they were married in Algiers.

While celebrating the publication of his book *Chooky,* John Faulkner posed with his sons, Jimmy and Chooky, and his wife Lucille. The portrait of Chooky in the background was painted by Maud Falkner.

115

M/S MINMAGARY
OXFORD

Hugh Evans, Master
Ross Brown, Mate
Ashford Little, M.D., Surgeon
Mary Evans, Cabin Boy

Port Watch
Maggie Brown

Starboard Watch
Minnie Ruth Little

Out of Confusion by Boundless Hope:

Conceived in a Canadian Club bottle She was born A.D. 15th August 1947 by ignominious Caesarean Section in prone position with her bottom upward in Evans's back yard eleven miles from the nearest water deeper than a half-inch kitchen tap & waxed & grew daily there beneath the whole town's exempt cynosure:

Whereupon there stood already on the horizon of her tender infancy Six Impassable Milestones:

1. They can't turn her over.
2. They can't find a truck big enough to haul her to water.
3. They can't load her onto the truck.
4. The truck can't turn the first corner outside the yard.
5. They can't get her off the truck into the water.
6. She will capsize or sink the moment her bottom is wet.

And waxed & grew & on the 7th January 1948 rose up & stood on her own bottom to receive the confirmation of her shiphood in deck & superstructure: & that was the First Milestone:

And waxed & grew: nor Rain nor Snow nor Ice nor Hail nor Storm nor Thaw nor Bonk of Night did slay that slow confused completion through power plant and pump and cleat and winch and hook & on the first day of June the truck arrived: & that was the Second Milestone:

And in the gloam of afternoon was raised tenderly in the myriad hands of her conceivers owners & artificers & their children friends well-wishers & dogs & the neighbors & merely curious & their friends & well-wishers & dogs: onto the truck: and that was the Third Milestone:

And at dawn's crack next morning the truck turned the first Impassable Corner: which was the Fourth Milestone: & at Three Bells in the Sixth Watch floated free from the launching ramp into deep water & was warped into moorings: and that was the Fifth and the Sixth Milestones:

And the Captain came aboard: at which moment she went into Commission: of which it is hereby decreed and avowed that any and all Panola County nations bordering that Oxford Ocean contumelously maliciously & feloniously miscalled Sardis Dam take cognizance of these Letters of Marque, and BEWARE

Given under my Hand & Seal
This Day Anno Domini
2nd June 1948
William Faulkner
First Sea Lord
Lafayette County Mississippi

From 1947 to 1948 Faulkner was periodically engaged in the pleasant pastime of building a houseboat with his friends, Dr. Ashford Little, Ross Brown, and Colonel Hugh Evans. They christened the craft *Minmagary*, combining the names of the friends' wives (Minnie Ruth, Maggie and Mary). Faulkner spent many happy weeks in the spring of 1948 helping to outfit and furnish the houseboat, which was launched at Sardis Reservoir, 18 miles northwest to Oxford. Having formally drawn up a "Letter of Marque," he commissioned the *Minmagary* as a "Ship of the Line in the Provisional Navy of the Confederate States of America," whose home waters he called "Oxford Ocean."

By virtue of whatever authority I may have inherited from my Great Grandfather. William C. Falkner Colonel (PAROLED) Second Mississippi Infantry Provisional Army Confederate States of America I William C Falkner II reposing all trust & confidence in the staunchness & stability of M/S Minmagary & in the courage & fidelity of her officers & crew do by these presents constitute & appoint her to be a Ship of the Line in the Provisional Navy of the Confederate States of America & further direct that all seamen soldiers & civilians recognising the above authority recognise her as such & accord her all the priviledges respect & consideration of that state & condition.

Given under my Great Grandfather's sword this Twenty Fourth July 1948 at Oxford Mississippi

William C Falkner II

At a party during the construction of the *Minmagary,* Colonel Hugh Evans took a photograph which Faulkner later claimed to be his favorite. The picture was made one year after publication of Malcolm Cowley's *Portable Faulkner,* an anthology which had greatly enhanced Faulkner's reputation in America, especially on university campuses. At this point in his career, Faulkner had completed much of his fiction: seventeen out of an eventual twenty-six major works.

Town and County

Faulkner raised mules on his 320-acre farm about 17 miles northeast of Oxford. With the help of his brother, John, he bred mules and grew corn to feed them. In some of his works he gave the mule a significant role as a symbol of strength, endurance, and humility. Cofield recalls, "Bill Faulkner saw Phil Mullen's closeup picture of a Mississippi mule in my studio one day — I had attached to the print a clipping of his writings in praise of the lowly mule. He said, 'Looks good off by itself' — meaning his description of the mule — 'Want me to sign it for you?' And he autographed it right there. Only time I ever saw him autograph something without being asked."

Photographs taken at the turn of the century record the facades of two general stores in Lafayette County. The store on the right was located at College Hill Community across the road from the church where William Faulkner married Estelle Oldham. It served the citizens of this small hamlet as general store, post office, and polling place.

At the country store farmers obtained news, gossip, and jokes, along with staple goods and farming equipment.

The Tankersley family home, photographed at the turn of the century, was located northwest of Oxford in the general vicinity of Faulkner's fictional "Sutpen's Hundred."

Even after the turn of the century, the success of Lafayette County's agrarian economy depended upon the abundance of inexpensive labor furnished chiefly by blacks.

The old Yocona River bridge, photographed in the early 1900's, was one of several covered bridges in Lafayette County. Local residents pronounced the Indian name Yocona, "Yok-nee."

Approximately ten miles southeast of Oxford, an old iron bridge spans the Yocona River. According to the map Faulkner drew of his Yoknapatawpha County, the location of this bridge corresponds to the one in *As I Lay Dying*.

A picture of the Yocona River at flood stage recalls the struggles of the Bundren family to cross the swollen river which was its fictional counterpart in *As I Lay Dying*.

Most children of rural Lafayette County were too isolated by poor roads and distance to attend the Oxford Public Schools. This small country school, which typified the "one room" system found throughout the county in the early 1900's, also resembled the school in *The Hamlet* that Eula Varner attended.

About eight miles south of Oxford is the crossroads community of Taylor, a thriving town in the 1800's, where trains were loaded with cotton grown in the rich river bottom. Faulkner, who loved the railroad, often rode the train to Taylor as a youth, then hiked back to Oxford. In his novel *Sanctuary* he has Temple Drake step off the train to meet Gowan Stevens at Taylor.

The old Shipp house was located close to Taylor. Cofield remarks, "I've always thought Bill used it as a model for the 'Old Frenchman's Place.'"

128

The typical farmer of Lafayette County plowed the hills to eke out a subsistence; however, some of the bottom land along the creeks and rivers furnished rich soil for the growing of cotton. In the 1940's, Phil Mullen's camera recorded this scene of black field hands at work on a large farm near Oxford (opposite page).

In another photograph by Mullen taken on a hot autumn day in the 1940's, farmers patiently waited their turn in cotton wagons outside the Avent Gin.

129

A picture of North Lamar looking toward the square was taken from the front yard of the old Murry Falkner home. From the opposite side of the square, the courthouse cupola dominated the skyline. (Photo taken in the 1920's.)

The old Federal Building, erected in 1885, stood across the street from the First National Bank. Still a notable landmark in Oxford (recently restored as City Hall), this building housed the U.S. Federal Court for the North Mississippi District.

In a scene of the Lafayette County Courthouse photographed in the early 1930's (opposite page), some of the balconied stores are visible in the background. (Note the wood-paneled bus partially obscured by the automobile in the foreground.)

Faulkner once remarked to Cofield that his favorite picture of the courthouse was the one taken from the balcony above Blaylock's Drugstore on the south side of the square.

Dr. John Culley's antebellum home was the setting for *So Red the Rose,* a novel by another Oxford writer, Stark Young. Local legend also associated this old house with the fictional home of Emily Grierson in Faulkner's "A Rose for Emily."

Two years before "A Rose for Emily" was written, the city fathers had contracted with the Barber Construction Company to undertake a paving project similar to the one mentioned in the story. The company foreman became very popular in Oxford and was nicknamed "Cap'n Jack."

132

In describing two important settings in *Light in August* Faulkner may have been thinking of St. Peter's Church and the Oxford City Jail. Though Faulkner did not regularly attend church services, family events such as weddings and christenings were held at historic St. Peter's. The city jail (now demolished) was for years a local landmark. With ornate molded eaves and attractive facade it looked more like a residence than a jail.

Faulkner posed for Phil Mullen with some of his deer hunting friends. Cofield notes, "No doubt they were discussing the cold, cold trail of long ago. From left: 'Red' Brite, John Cullen (back to camera), Faulkner, Ike Roberts and Bill Evans."

Covering local news for the *Oxford Eagle*, Phil Mullen photographed a political rally on the square. A string band warmed up the crowd of spectators before the arrival of the candidate for the United States Senate, Judge John Stennis.

Faulkner watched a parade around Oxford's square staged for the benefit of a Ford Foundation film. In the right foreground he stands beside a flat-bed trailer, dressed in dark suit and hat with a white handkerchief in his pocket.

On less eventful days, a common sight on the shady courthouse lawn was the serious faces of domino players.

"Saturday was the busiest day of the week," Cofield recalls, "and Oxford's square attracted some 'blaring' sermons from traveling evangelists" (opposite page).

The courthouse lawn was a place where one could meet friends and pass the time of day, or even transact business. Spring, summer, and fall, farmers set up rough stalls to sell their produce. Watermelons came into season in mid-July, and the price of a large melon in the 1940's was about ten cents.

A studio portrait of "Colonel" Cofield was made in Oxford by his father, John Isaac Cofield, of Cordele, Georgia. A professional photographer himself, the elder Mr. Cofield visited his son every fall to help him retouch negatives of the hundreds of photographs he took for *Ole Miss,* the school yearbook.

Phil Mullen was photographed by Cofield in the late 1940's not long after having been discharged from the armed services and having returned to Oxford. As editor of the *Oxford Eagle,* Mullen was a leader in civic affairs and an active promoter of his town and its citizens.

"On occasion, Phil Mullen asked me to critique his news photos," Cofield notes. "We'd go in the darkroom at my studio and print his pictures. (In this case it was some parade or July 4th or something.) Phil was always hustling and bustling around the county taking pictures and writing news stories. This shot of Phil and me was taken by my son, Jack."

138

Cofield recounts a story told to him by W. M. "Mac" Reed, partner in Gathright-Reed Drugstore, about an incident which occurred in the early 1930's: "Bill came into the drugstore one evening, all cut up and bleeding like a stuck pig, and told Mac, 'Well, I at last did it — I deliberately ran my car into a telephone pole. It was running away with me, and I had lost control; so I headed for the pole and hit it dead center.' Mac took him back of the prescription counter, and proceeded to doctor his numerous cuts received from flying glass. The merthiolate burned like the dickens on the raw cuts, and Bill was cussin' up a storm, so bad in fact that Mac had to 'call him down' and threaten to ask the local constable, who happened to be standing in front of the store, to calm him down. Bill said, 'Hell, I'd rather spend the night in jail than to be burned alive!' Finally, Mac called Phil Stone, and he came and got Bill and drove him home (a-fuming all the way). It seems Bill recovered very nicely without any undue scars or broken bones, and the next day he was all regrets. Forgiveness was asked from all quarters and freely given, as everyone knew this was so unlike friend Bill, he being the most unassuming fellow in these parts."

139

Random House published
Faulkner's *Intruder in the Dust*
in 1948, and M.G.M. purchased
film rights to the novel about
racial tensions. When director
Clarence Brown brought his film
crew and actors to Oxford the
following spring to begin film
production, Faulkner showed
mixed emotions about
participating in promotion of
the movie. Asked to pose for a
publicity photograph, he at first
refused, then grudgingly agreed
to allow Mullen to take his
picture, though he insisted upon
posing "as he was" — wearing
work clothes, a tweed coat, and
an uncompromising expression.

During the filming, Mullen
photographed a scene on the
square. The townspeople
enjoyed the excitement and
glamor of movie-making, and
William Faulkner's local
reputation was considerably
enhanced. The Falkner family,
and especially Miss Maud, also
enjoyed the novelty of film
production in Oxford.

Local studio portraits of Hollywood actors included Claude Jarman, young lead actor in "Intruder," and Porter Hall, veteran character actor.

For publicity purposes Phil Mullen caught actor David Brian in an impromptu pose at the desk of the Colonial Hotel. Mullen also photographed Will Geer, who played the sheriff in the film with Lafayette County Sheriff Boyce Bratton (left) and former sheriff, Ike Roberts.

"Intruder in the Dust" premiered in Oxford at the Lyric Theatre in October of 1949 to a standing-room-only house. The excited crowd gathered outside the Lyric to await the arrival of honored guests: Faulkner and his family, director Clarence Brown and the actors, and local officials led by Mayor Bob Williams.

After the film, reporters pressed Faulkner for his comment, which was favorable, though the author had threatened earlier that day not to attend the premiere at all. However, family members had pleaded, cajoled, and at last coerced him into attendance.

Cofield comments on two of
Faulkner's friends in Oxford:
"Felix Linder was Bill's
childhood friend and later was
his family doctor for many
years. And Bill's old friend,
Phil Stone, gave him a lifetime
of friendship and support. My
son Jack took this portrait of
Stone sitting on a bench on the
Ole Miss campus."

Cofield photographed Judge John Falkner in his law office on the square. He recalls his first meeting with William's uncle: "I stepped upstairs one day in 1928 — back of the old First National Bank — to see Judge John W. T. Falkner, something about legal business regarding my studio, and in the conversation I casually asked the Judge if he happened to be any kin to William Faulkner. He blurted out, 'What, that nut! I'm sorry to say he's my newphew.' A few years later he lived to eat those words, eh?"

Judge Taylor McElroy was mayor of Oxford for many years and later became a state Supreme Court Justice. Early in McElroy's career, Faulkner helped him run for election by barnstorming and dropping leaflets on a political rally at Ripley.

145

Cofield explains the circumstances of a picture taken of William and his brother John in 1949: "John and Bill Faulkner's only picture together (as grown men) was made by Phil Mullen in front of John's house. William had loaned John his new lawnmower to spruce up his front yard on the occasion of a visit from his son Jimmy's future wife, Nan. Since Bill hadn't heard from John for about a week, he went to get his lawnmower back (along with the gasoline funnel he's holding in his hand). Phil Mullen happened to be driving by, saw them together, jumped out and asked them to pose." The photograph was taken several months before William was notified that he had won the Nobel Prize for Literature.

SVENSKA AKADEMIEN

HAR VID SAMMANTRÄDE DEN 10 NOVEMBER 1950
I ÖVERENSSTÄMMELSE MED FÖRESKRIFTERNA
I DET AV

ALFRED NOBEL

DEN 27 NOVEMBER 1895 UPPRÄTTADE TESTAMENTE
BESLUTAT ATT TILLDELA

Estelle said goodbye to William and Jill at Memphis Airport on December 6, 1950, as they left for New York en route to Stockholm, where Faulkner was to accept the Nobel Prize for Literature. On November 10, 1950, Faulkner had received a telephone call in Oxford notifying him that the Swedish Academy had awarded him the 1949 Nobel Prize. Although he was proud of this achievement, he was reluctant to leave his cherished privacy in Oxford and travel to Sweden to accept his award. A determined family conference, however, resulted in a plan to get him to go. Estelle's argument was especially convincing. She asked William to give Jill an opportunity to travel to Europe.

149

On December 8, Faulkner and his daughter boarded a Scandinavian Airlines plane at New York's La Guardia Airport for the final leg of their journey to Sweden. Accompanying newsmen photographed William and Jill seated aboard the plane. During the flight William worked on a draft of his acceptance speech.

At the awards ceremony in Stockholm, Faulkner was seated next to Bertrand Russell, who had won the 1950 Nobel Prize for Literature.

150

Faulkner and Russell received their awards from King Gustaf Adolf of Sweden. In addition to the Nobel certificate and medal, they received a cash award of $30,000.00.

In the spring of 1951, William and Estelle gave a party for Jill and her classmates to celebrate their graduation from high school. Phil Mullen took this photograph for the *Oxford Eagle* to publicize the commemoration address which Faulkner had agreed to give at the graduation exercises.

As Nobel Laureate, Faulkner was highly sought after by many institutions as guest lecturer, yet he refused all of them in the months immediately following his acceptance of the Nobel Prize — all, that is, except the request of his daughter, Jill. The photograph was taken by Phil Mullen during a Ford Foundation film re-enacting the graduation exercises.

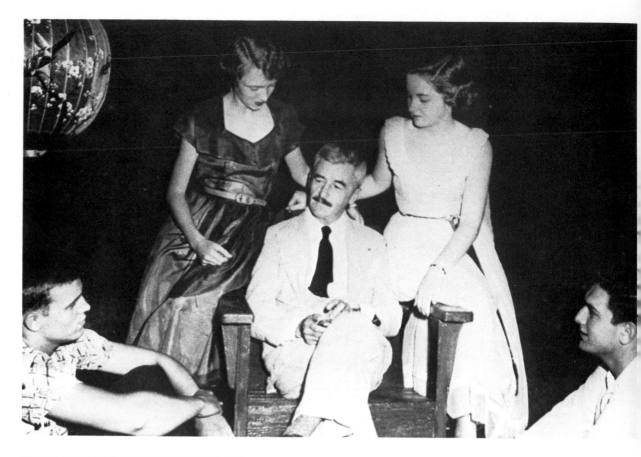

154

Out of the public eye, Faulkner
loved to sail his nineteen foot
sailboat, *The Ring Dove*, at
Sardis Reservoir near Oxford.
He bought the boat from Arthur
Guyton for $300.00 and took it
home to Rowan Oak, where he
spent weeks scraping, caulking,
painting, and fitting it for
launching.

155

Faulkner was invited to speak at the 1952 Delta Council meeting in Cleveland, Mississippi. His most recent major publications were *Collected Stories* (1950) and *Requiem for a Num* (1951). Joining him after the program was his old friend and former literary agent, Ben Wasson.

During a break in the program, photographer Bern Keating found Faulkner and Wasson relaxing. Another picture (opposite page) caught Faulkner in a reflective mood.

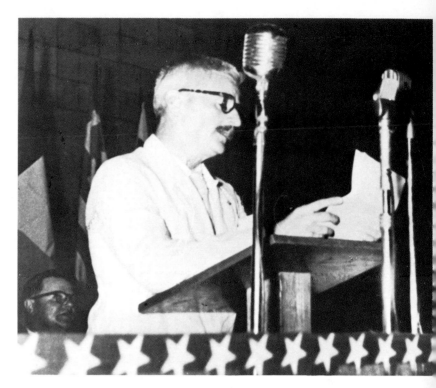

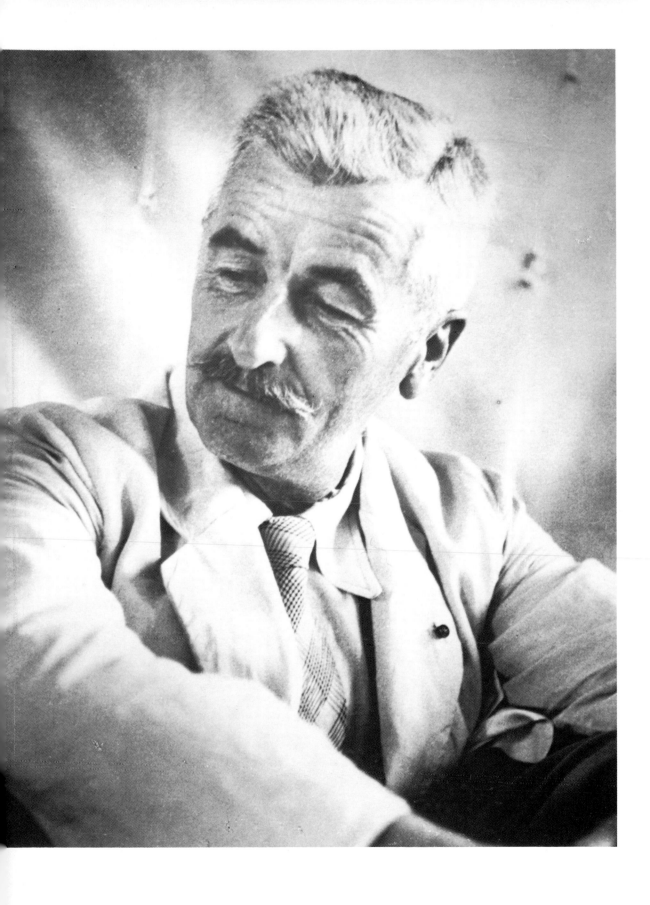

In 1952 the Ford Foundation
commissioned a short
biographical film about
Faulkner. During film sequences
set at Rowan Oak, Faulkner and
director Howard Maywood
discussed the script in the
writer's library.

During the filming, Mullen took
a picture of Phil Stone and
Faulkner at Stone's law office.
Another picture by Mullen
recorded a film scene in
Gathright-Reed Drugstore on
the square, showing Faulkner
talking with his friend,
W. M. "Mac" Reed.

159

Jill Faulkner was engaged to be married to Paul Summers of Rockville, Maryland, in 1954. On August 21, 1954, Faulkner accompanied his daughter into St. Peter's Episcopal Church, where he gave her away in marriage to Summers. At Rowan Oak, he toasted his daughter with champagne.

When the Warner Brothers film "Land of the Pharaohs" was previewed in Memphis in 1955, Faulkner and Jill posed for a publicity photograph with representatives of the studio. Faulkner had written the screenplay for director Howard Hawks and had traveled to location sites in Egypt during the filming of the epic motion picture.

At the Memphis preview of "Land of the Pharaohs" were family members (from left) Malcolm Franklin, his wife, Gloria, Mrs. Jack Falkner, Paul Summers, Jill, William, Estelle, Jack, and Mrs. Walter B. McLean ("Aunt Bama").

163

In 1955, the year Faulkner won
a Pulitzer Prize for his novel
A Fable, William and Estelle
posed for U.P.I. photographers
in front of Rowan Oak. Reporters
also were pressing Faulkner to
comment on the current civil
rights question.

164

Faulkner did much of his writing in the study which he built after he won the Nobel Prize. Cofield describes an interesting feature of the "office," as Faulkner called it: "Guess just about everybody's heard the story about the notes Bill printed on his office wall when he was writing *A Fable*. He wrote the outline of the different events for different weekdays up to 'Tomorrow,' which he put in the corner on the other side of the door."

Behind Rowan Oak, William and Estelle designed and planted a formal garden, with grass walks separating rose gardens surrounded by privet hedges. In the left foreground a circular bench encloses a wisteria vine. Rowan Oak is barely visible behind the high shrubs.

165

In the paddock which he himself built at Rowan Oak, Faulkner kept several horses that he rode daily for exercise and relaxation. Concerning Faulkner's treatment of his horses, Cofield comments, "Bill's jumper Tempy was one of his favorites — and he surely spent a lot of time with his horses. He had a way with horse-flesh, had the patience of Job doctoring his saddle-horses at Rowan Oak (or his mules at his farm). If he hadn't been a writer, he'd have made one heck of a veterinarian!"

Each spring, Faulkner also
enjoyed getting his sailboat
ready for the coming season.

In May, 1955, Faulkner went
to Cofield for a picture to use
in a passport for his State
Department tour of Japan
scheduled for July of that year.
About Faulkner's appearance
Cofield remarks, "I never saw a
fellow that could go to such
absolute extremes in wearing-
apparel and general appearance.
One day you meet him and he
looks just like he'd stepped off
an Illinois Central box-car. The
next time he greets you in attire
that would outdo the late Prince
of Wales!"

During his tour of Japan as
Goodwill Ambassador for the
United States, Faulkner posed
with the Nagano seminar group.

168

After his successful but exhausting three-week tour of Japan, Faulkner went to the Philippines for a visit with his stepdaughter, Victoria, and her family. In the snapshot, Faulkner is shown relaxing with Victoria's husband, Bill Fielden, and Vicki, their daughter. In another photo, Victoria and Vicki are pictured at their home, where Faulkner stayed for two days before leaving for the next stop on his State Department tour — Rome.

Not long after his return from the fatiguing State Department tour, William was hospitalized in Memphis for a bleeding ulcer. Dr. Richard B. Crowder took several pictures of him. He had been suffering from a back injury sustained in a fall from his horse. As had previously been the case with similar injuries, Faulkner drank to ease the pain. Added to these physical ailments was his frustration over the civil rights crisis and the fact that people, both in the North and the South, misinterpreted his moderate views. The combination of injuries, emotions, and drinking resulted in a bleeding ulcer, which continued to plague him for the remaining six years of his life.

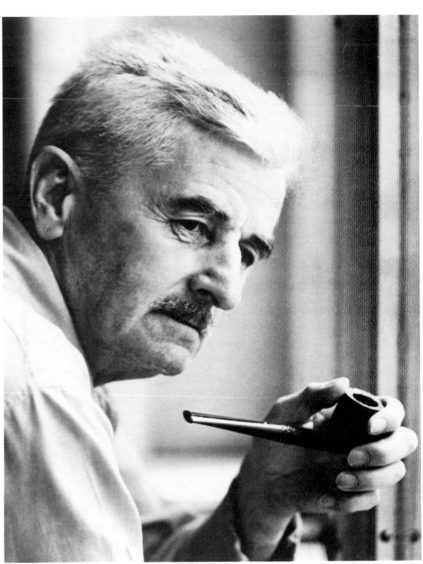

In April, 1956, while Faulkner was still convalescing, Cofield decided to photograph Rowan Oak: "I wanted to get a shot of it with the rays of the sun peeping through those ancient cedars. Drove over to Bill's place at daybreak, got my view camera set up, ducked under the black hood and focused on the house. Before I took the exposure I could feel someone behind me! Bill Faulkner had sneaked up behind me (he was supposed to be sick in bed!), grinning at being able to do it without making a sound. I just shook my head. Bill said, 'Mawnin, Cofield.'"

172

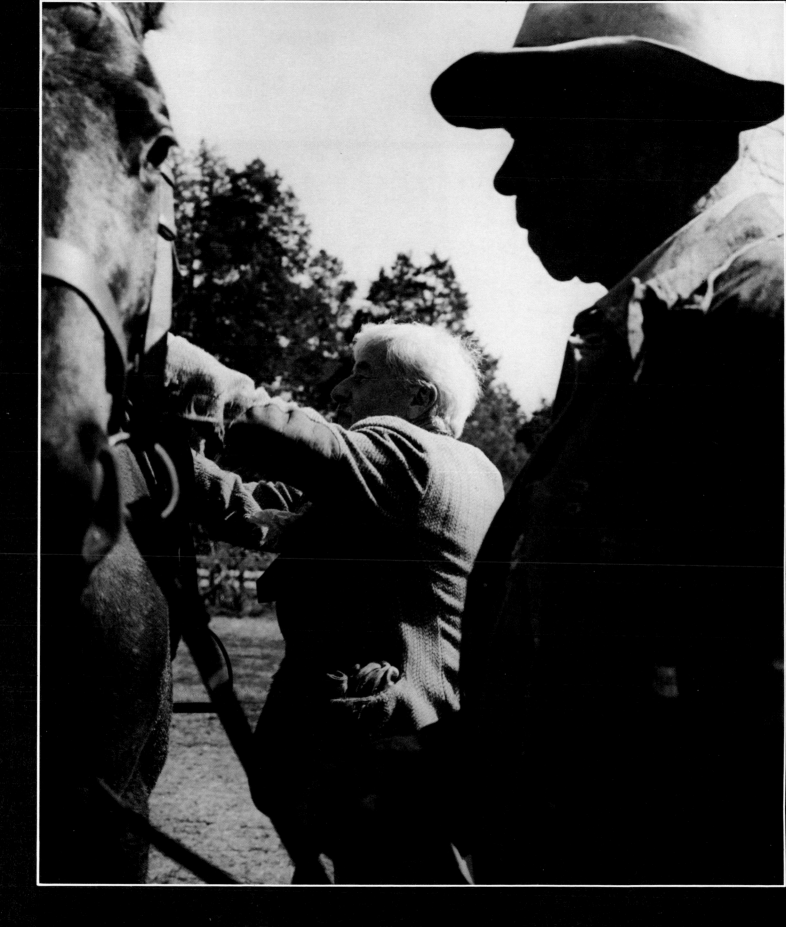

Man of Letters

Faulkner finished writing the second novel of his Snopes trilogy, *The Town*, in 1956, and spent many months alternating his time between Oxford and New York. In addition to his own work and related activities, he had been appointed by President Eisenhower to participate in the "People-to-People" program, which was created to improve understanding between nations during the Cold War period. *(Photo by Phyllis Wagner)*

175

Faulkner joined the staff of the University of Virginia as writer-in-residence in February, 1957. Ralph Thompson photographed Faulkner standing beside the pillars of Cabell Hall.

Among his pleasant times in Charlottesville, Virginia, were visits with his new grandson, Paul D. "Tad" Summers III. He also enjoyed hunting trips in Virginia, occasionally accompanied by his daughter, Jill.

In 1959, Faulkner purchased a house on Rugby Road in Charlottesville within walking distance of the University. During his tenure there, his play *Requiem for a Nun* had its Broadway premiere, and Random House published the third novel of his Snopes trilogy, *The Mansion*. From 1958 to 1959 Faulkner's literary agent, Harold Ober, helped negotiate for him the sale of screen rights to *The Sound and the Fury* and *Light in August*, as well as dramatic rights to *Requiem for a Nun*.

Faulkner's primary responsibility at the University of Virginia was to talk with students and faculty about literature, especially his own work. When the photograph was taken, he was fielding questions during a session at McGregor Hall.

In the summer of 1958, Faulkner left Charlottesville and returned to Oxford to make arrangements for a second wedding party, that of his niece and ward, Dean. Posing with Dean during the reception at Rowan Oak, he was dapper and cheerful despite severly bruised ribs sustained in a fall from his jumper, Tempy, the day before the wedding.

Receiving wedding guests at Rowan Oak, Faulkner reserved a special smile for Dean's uncle and aunt, Roger and Clara Caldwell. About this picture, Cofield later noted, "Best smiling photo I ever took of Bill."

Proud of his horse, Tempy, Faulkner requested a series of photographs to be made in the paddock adjacent to his home. The author also posed with his groom, Andrew Price, a man of dignity and loyalty. Price worked for Faulkner for many years, living in the servants quarters behind Rowan Oak with his wife, Chrissie, who was Estelle's housekeeper. Faulkner and Price held each other in mutual esteem and one of William's horses was maintained exclusively for Andrew.

The camera captured Faulkner's determined expression as he brought Tempy over a low jump. Throughout many years of training Tempy and other horses, Faulkner experienced occasional painful bruises and some very serious back injuries.

Dr. Chester McLarty was one of several Oxford physicians who attended to Faulkner's medical needs.

182

Faulkner spent the summer of 1960 in Oxford, returning to his duties at the University of Virginia in the fall. During his vacation he rode his horses, did minor chores about Rowan Oak and his farm in the country, and sailed *The Ring Dove* at Sardis. As always, his country squire role in Oxford contrasted sharply with his international image as a man of letters.

His literary awards included the Nobel and Pulitzer prizes, the Gold Medal Award of the National Institute of Arts and Letters, the American Academy's Howell's Medal for Fiction, the National Book Award, the Legion of Honor, the Silver Medal of the Greek Academy, and the Order of Andres Bello (pictured). He gave all his prizes to his mother, who kept them in a box in her bedroom.

184

Maud Butler Falkner died on October 6, 1960, at the age of 88. True to her independent and self-reliant nature, she had asked that no glucose or other artificial stimulants be given her to sustain life when the end was obvious. She had also given explicit funeral instructions — no embalming, a pine box, and immediate burial — saying, "I want to get back to earth as fast as I can."

The United States Military Academy invited Faulkner to pay a two-day visit to West Point in April, 1962. He was accompanied by his wife, his daughter, and his son-in-law, Paul Summers, a West Point graduate. While photographers' shutters clicked, Faulkner read from his last novel, *The Reivers*.

Cofield recalls an exchange Faulkner had with a cadet during his trip to West Point:

"One cadet asked him something to the effect: 'Why, Mr. Faulkner, do you use so much backwoods dialect and so many *aints* mixed in with your perfect English?' Quoth he, 'I happen to be the world's oldest sixth-grader.' (Truth is, he *was* mainly self-taught and always kept his Webster's handy at home, same as the parson with his Good Book.)"

At home in Oxford, Faulkner enjoyed relaxing with his horses. A snapshot taken by a neighbor showed Faulkner's gentle touch with his animals. Ironically, it was a fall from one of his horses which precipitated his death.

Morris Warman

On June 17, 1962, Faulkner suffered a fall from his horse, Stonewall, taking the brunt of the impact on his back. In the twenty days of his life remaining to him, he would experience pain both lying and sitting. The back brace that he had occasionally worn during the past six months gave little relief. No pills, injections, or whiskey could stem the pain. On July 5, he was taken to a private clinic at Byhalia, Mississippi, where he was treated for complications arising from his back injury. Early the next morning Faulkner was stricken with a totally unexpected heart attack and died of a coronary thrombosis.

In Memory

of

William Faulkner

This Business Will Be

Closed

From 2:00 To 2:15 P.M.

Today, July 7, 1962

In keeping with the Falkner
tradition, the family issued an
appeal for privacy: "Until he is
buried he belongs to the family.
After that he belongs to the
world."

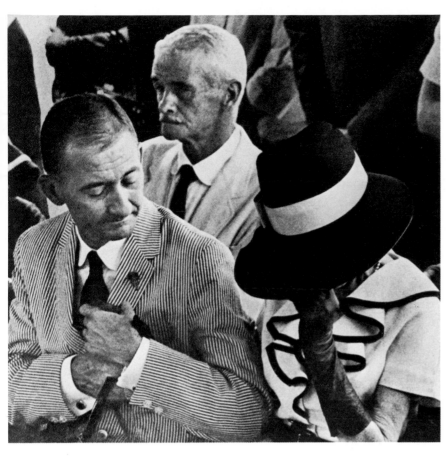

During the brief graveside ceremony, William's stepson, Malcolm Franklin, comforted his mother. Seated behind them was William's brother, John.

Followed by the family members, pallbearers carried the coffin to the grave past William's old friends, Mac Reed and Phil Stone.

Appended to the back of one of Cofield's framed portraits of Faulkner is this typewritten note: "I once read a statement by Rudyard Kipling (made, I think, in one of his last interviews in London), which I think applies to Bill Faulkner the *man* as well as William Faulkner the *author:* 'The individual has always had to struggle to keep from being overwhelmed by the tribe. To be your own man is a hard business. If you try it you'll be lonely often, and sometimes frightened. But no price is too high to pay for the privilege of owning yourself.' Bill Faulkner lived up to this principle to a *T.*"

Falkner Genealogy

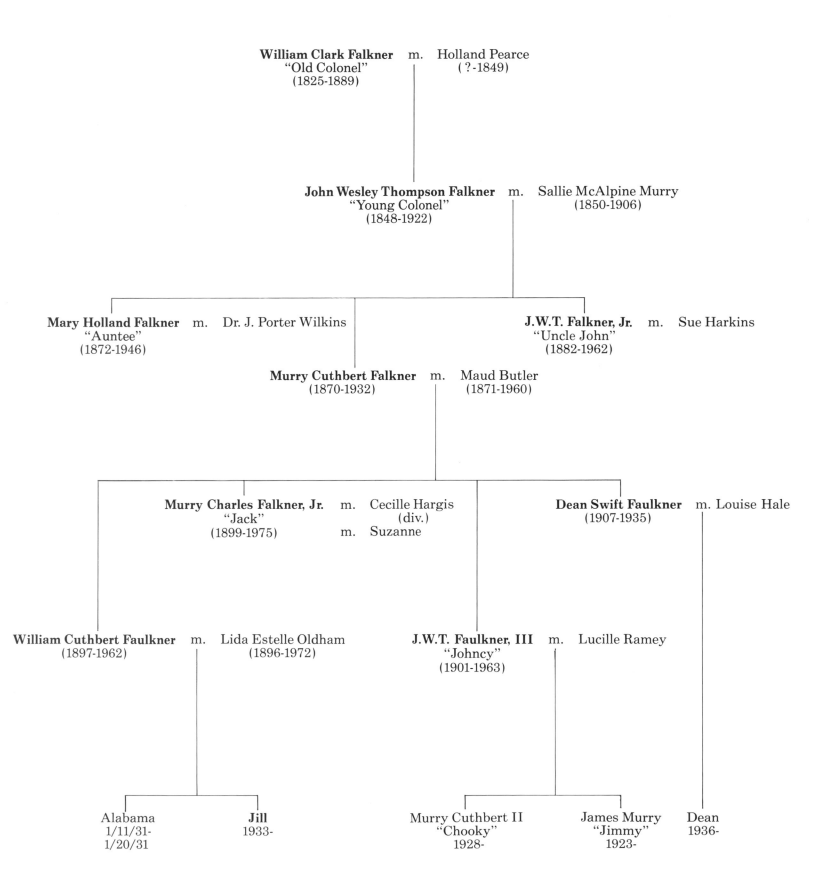

William Clark Falkner   m.   Holland Pearce
"Old Colonel"   (?-1849)
(1825-1889)

John Wesley Thompson Falkner   m.   Sallie McAlpine Murry
"Young Colonel"   (1850-1906)
(1848-1922)

Mary Holland Falkner   m.   Dr. J. Porter Wilkins   J.W.T. Falkner, Jr.   m.   Sue Harkins
"Auntee"   "Uncle John"
(1872-1946)   (1882-1962)

Murry Cuthbert Falkner   m.   Maud Butler
(1870-1932)   (1871-1960)

Murry Charles Falkner, Jr.   m.   Cecille Hargis   Dean Swift Faulkner   m. Louise Hale
"Jack"   (div.)   (1907-1935)
(1899-1975)   m.   Suzanne

William Cuthbert Faulkner   m.   Lida Estelle Oldham   J.W.T. Faulkner, III   m.   Lucille Ramey
(1897-1962)   (1896-1972)   "Johncy"
                                          (1901-1963)

Alabama   Jill   Murry Cuthbert II   James Murry   Dean
1/11/31-   1933-   "Chooky"   "Jimmy"   1936-
1/20/31   1928-   1923-

Acknowledgments

P. 17: Falkner home, courtesy William Boozer Collection; p. 18: courtesy Mrs. J. E. Woodward; pp. 19, 20, 21: courtesy Dean F. Wells; p. 23: building, courtesy Aston Holley; p. 26: train, courtesy Tippah County Historical Society; p. 29: courtesy Dean F. Wells; p. 30: courtesy Mrs. Jamie T. Parker; p. 35: Maud with Murry and William, courtesy Dean F. Wells; p. 36: courtesy Dean F. Wells; p. 38: Dean Falkner, courtesy Mrs. Louise Meadow; p. 39: courtesy Dean F. Wells; p. 41; house, courtesy Mrs. William Baker; p. 43: courtesy Mrs. William Hall; p. 45: North Street, courtesy Mrs. William Hall; p. 49: picnic, courtesy Carvel Collins; p. 50: Estelle Oldham, courtesy The Mississippi Collection, University of Mississippi Library; William Faulkner, courtesy Mrs. Louise Meadow; p. 51: courtesy The Mississippi Collection; p. 52: house, courtesy Joe Blasingame; Phil Stone, courtesy The Mississippi Collection; p. 56: courtesy Dean F. Wells; p. 58: archway, courtesy The Mississippi Collection; p. 60: courtesy The Mississippi Collection; p. 61: courtesy Howard G. Duvall, Jr.; p. 62: courtesy The Mississippi Collection; p. 63: courtesy Dr. E. V. Bramlett; p. 64: train, courtesy Mrs. William Hall; pp. 65-66: courtesy The Mississippi Collection; p. 67: Murry C. Falkner, Jr., courtesy The Mississippi Collection; p. 68: building, courtesy The Mississippi Collection; sketch, courtesy Guy Turnbow, Jr.; p. 69: building, courtesy William Lester; p. 70: William Faulkner, courtesy George Healey; sketch, courtesy Dean F. Wells; p. 71: courtesy Carvel Collins; p. 72: courtesy Mrs. Thomas Leatherbury; p. 73: courtesy Mrs. James Black; p. 75: Ben Wasson, photo by Doris Ullman, courtesy Ben Wasson; p. 76: power plant, courtesy The Mississippi Collection; pp. 79-84: courtesy William Boozer Collection; p. 85: W. M. Reed, courtesy Aston Holley; p. 86: courtesy Greater Memphis Chamber of Commerce; p. 87: *Memphis Commercial Appeal*; p. 88: courtesy Joseph Blotner; p. 90: courtesy The Mississippi Collection; p. 91: courtesy Dean F. Wells; p. 92: courtesy The Mississippi Collection; p. 93: Jill Faulkner, courtesy Dean F. Wells; William and Jill, courtesy Joseph Blotner; p. 95: courtesy William Boozer Collection; pp. 96-97: courtesy Faulkner family; p. 98: courtesy Mrs. Louise Meadow; p. 99: Dean Falkner, courtesy Mrs. Louise Meadow; p. 100: courtesy The Mississippi Collection; p. 101: photo by Dan Brennan; p. 103: Caroline Barr and Dean Falkner, courtesy Dean F. Wells; Louise and Dean, courtesy Mrs. Louise Meadow; p. 104: courtesy Dean F. Wells; p. 107: William Faulkner, by Dan Brennan; p. 108: photos by Dan Brennan; p. 109: house and car, by Dan Brennan; gazebo, courtesy William Boozer Collection; pp. 110-111: photos by Dan Brennan; pp. 112-113: courtesy Mrs. John Faulkner; p. 114: courtesy Joseph Blotner; p. 115: Faulkner and Ruth Ford, *Memphis Commercial Appeal*; Murry and wife, John and family, courtesy Faulkner family; pp. 117-118: courtesy Dr. and Mrs. Ashford Little; pp. 119, 121: courtesy Phil Mullen; p. 122: store exteriors, courtesy Aston Holley; store interior, courtesy Phil Mullen; p. 123: courtesy Joe Blasingame; p. 124: covered bridge, courtesy Aston Holley; p. 125: courtesy Phil Mullen; p. 127: Taylor Depot, courtesy Mrs. N. B. Jones; pp. 128-129: courtesy Phil Mullen; p. 130: courthouse, courtesy Joe Blasingame; p. 136: courtesy Joe Blasingame; p. 137: jail, courtesy University of Tennessee Library; pp. 134-137: courtesy Phil Mullen; p. 139: drugstore, courtesy William Lester; W. M. Reed, courtesy Susie James; p. 144; courtesy Phil Mullen; p. 145: David Brian at hotel, Will Geer with sheriffs, courtesy Phil Mullen; pp. 142-143: courtesy The Mississippi Collection; p. 144: Dr. Felix Linder, courtesy Phil Mullen; p. 146: courtesy Phil Mullen; pp. 149, 150: *Memphis Commercial Appeal*; p. 151: Faulkner and Jill, courtesy Faulkner family; Faulkner at Nobel Prize ceremony, courtesy Joseph Blotner; p. 152: courtesy Faulkner family; pp. 154-155: courtesy Phil Mullen; p. 156: courtesy Bern Keating; p. 157: courtesy Carvel Collins; pp. 158-159: courtesy Phil Mullen; pp. 160-161: courtesy Mrs. Paul D. Summers, Jr.; p. 162: *Memphis Commercial Appeal*; p. 163: courtesy William Boozer Collection; p. 164: United Press International; p. 166: William Faulkner, *Memphis Commercial Appeal*; p. 167: United Press International; p. 168: Faulkner with Japanese, courtesy Carvel Collins; p. 169: Faulkner with Fieldens, courtesy Dean F. Wells; Victoria and Vicki Fielden, courtesy Doxie K. Williford; pp. 170-171: photos by Dr. Richard B. Crowder, courtesy Dean F. Wells; p. 173: courtesy Edwin B. Meek; p. 175: photo by Phyllis Cerf Wagner; p. 176: Faulkner at Cabell Hall, photo by Ralph Thompson, courtesy University of Virginia Library; Faulkner and Jill, courtesy Joseph Blotner; Faulkner and grandson, courtesy Dean F. Wells; p. 177: house, courtesy Yvonne Blotner; Faulkner lecturing, photo by R. C. Payne, courtesy University of Virginia Library; p. 182: Dr. McLarty, courtesy Dr. and Mrs. Chester McLarty; p. 183: courtesy Edwin E. Meek; p. 185: courtesy Dean F. Wells; p. 186: photos by Vytas Valaitis; p. 187: Faulkner with horse, courtesy Mrs. William Baker; p. 188: photo by Morris Warman; p. 189: typewriter, courtesy Patrick D. Smith; funeral notice, courtesy Howard G. Duvall, Jr.; p. 191: Malcolm Franklin and Estelle Faulkner, *Life*.

Faulkner's "pride and joy"
"Tippin"

He raised this(self taught)
"jumping horse" from a colt.
The horse i now 6 yrs. old.
(photos made May 1958)

Mr. & Mrs. William Faulkner entertain with(a so-called)
"Hunting Party" in Spring of 1938.
(depicted from left to right; front row- Dr. Tiley(author,
Emory University)-Mrs. J. C. Culley-Mrs. A. H. Little-
Bob Williams-Col. Evans(U.S. Army)-Mrs. Bob Williams-Mrs.
Felix Linder- Mr. & Mrs. Ross Brown, Sr. and Dr. J.C.Culley.
Back row-Mr. William Falkner, Mrs. Falkner and wee daughter
"Jill", with servants.
*Note-The old butler in center had his standing order to
serve jiggers of "Ole Forester" at every 30-minute
interval(you took it straight, no chasers allowed).

AT ROWAN OAKS
MAY '58

AT HOME
MAY '58